Child Care and Mediating Structures

A Conference Sponsored by the
American Enterprise Institute for Public Policy Research

Child Care and Mediating Structures

Edited by Brigitte Berger and Sidney Callahan

American Enterprise Institute for Public Policy Research
Washington, D.C.

Library of Congress Cataloging in Publication Data

Main entry under title:

Child care and mediating structures.

(AEI symposia ; 79G)
Includes bibliographical references.
1.   Child welfare—United States—Congresses.
I.   Berger, Brigitte.   II.   Callahan, Sidney Cornelia.
III.   American Enterprise Institute for Public Policy
Research.   IV.   Series: American Enterprise Institute
for Public Policy Research.   AEI symposia ; 79G.
HV741.C477   362.7′0973   79-17710
ISBN 0-8447-2162-X
ISBN 0-8447-2183-8 pbk.

AEI Symposia 79G

Printed in the United States of America

List of Participants

Mary Jo Bane
Graduate School of Education
Harvard University

Bertram M. Beck
Community Service Society

Brigitte Berger
Professor of Sociology
Wellesley College

Peter L. Berger
Department of Sociology
Boston College

George Brand
Lutheran Church in America

Barry Bruce-Briggs
Author

Sidney Callahan
Author and Psychologist

Audrey Cohen
College for Human Services

Constance Gaynor
Religious Leaders Program
University of Notre Dame

Myron Gershberg
New York City Department of Mental Health

Arlene Gilbert
Consultant

Peter Skerry
Mediating Structures Project

Margaret Steinfels
Hastings Center

Michael Szenberg
Department of Economics
Long Island University, Brooklyn Campus

Robert Woodson
American Enterprise Institute

Luitgard Wundheiler
Psychologist

Dennis Young
Averell Harriman School of Public Policy
State University of New York, Stony Brook

Contents

Preface

Contemporary society is rich in studies, conferences, debates, commissions, and policy formulations concerning children and their families. The United Nations has proclaimed 1979 as the International Year of the Child, and there have been several White House Conferences on Children in recent years. In fact, this era may well be remembered as the century of the child. Yet there is little agreement whether children receive more attention today than ever before, or whether they do not receive enough.

For instance, in one study of childhood citing reports from anthropologists and foreign visitors to the United States in the nineteenth century, the author observed: "We have set a new record; no other people seems ever to have been so preoccupied with children, so anxious about them or so uncertain about how to deal with them."[1] On the other hand, the Nestor of the study of children in contemporary society warns of a "national neglect of children" and maintains: "The evidence indicates that American society, whether viewed in comparison to other nations or to itself over time, is accordingly progressively less attentive to its children."[2]

This confusion is not peculiar to those who study the status and needs of children in America professionally; it is widespread throughout society as well. Individuals of all social classes and ethnic backgrounds are similarly ambiguous and uncertain whether the nation's children receive enough or too little attention, and whether the attention they do receive is beneficial and adequate. Nonetheless, the coexistence of views that children are both "pampered" and "neglected" and the urgent tone of the discussion reflect a profound concern for those who cannot care for themselves, among whom children hold the first place. In American society, this concern is so pronounced that

---

[1] Mary E. Goodman, *The Culture of Childhood: Child's Eye Views of Society and Culture* (New York: Teachers College Press, Columbia University, 1970).

[2] Urie Bronfenbrenner, in *White House Conference on Children* (Washington, D.C.: Government Printing Office, 1970).

foreign observers have been inclined to call it an obsession with children. With the proliferation of studies and the surfacing of ever more public advocates and guardians of ever more issues and causes, no cause has received more attention than the welfare of children. Children and their families have become an acute public issue.

In view of the attention that has been given to the child and family complex, it may appear superfluous to hold yet another conference, to present yet one more set of working papers, to formulate yet an additional theoretical basis from which public policy is to be guided. Yet, in spite of the heightened activities and fervently expressed compassionate commitments to the welfare of the nation's children, one position is strangely missing: the position of ordinary men and women. Although it has become fashionable in the emerging "post-reformist" mood to express proposals and policy suggestions in populist terms, the paradox remains that, when all is said and done, the values and hopes of a great many Americans are ignored.

The Mediating Structures Project of the American Enterprise Institute aims to remedy this neglect and to give voice to the concerns of individuals: its theme is "to empower people."[3] It aims to identify those institutions that have been disregarded, sometimes even to the verge of destruction, but that still continue to be of primary importance in the life of ordinary American citizens. These are institutions such as the family, neighborhood, church, and voluntary associations, and they are termed mediating structures. The further aim of the project is to explore the viability of these mediating structures, particularly in relation to the public institutions that have taken over many of their functions. A rethinking of the new and the old structures is called for.

Accordingly, on October 6 and 7, 1978, the Mediating Structures Project held a conference in New York City to explore the relation of mediating structures to public policy in the area of child care. The present volume contains three of the papers delivered at this conference, a report on the discussion, and reflections about the conference by the editors. The Mediating Structures Project is partially funded by a grant from the National Endowment for the Humanities.

PETER L. BERGER
RICHARD JOHN NEUHAUS
Codirectors
Mediating Structures Project

---

[3] See Peter L. Berger and Richard John Neuhaus, *To Empower People: The Role of Mediating Structures in Public Policy* (Washington, D.C.: American Enterprise Institute, 1977).

1
The Family and Mediating Structures as Agents for Child Care

Brigitte Berger

The term "mediating structures" refers to those institutions in contemporary society that stand between the individual's private life and the large institutions of the public sphere. Notable among them are the family, organized religion, voluntary associations, the neighborhood, and the ethnic or racial subculture. Among the mediating structures that order the life of most individuals the family holds a primary place. It is the most fundamental institution, not only linking the individual to all other institutions but in turn linking most institutions within its own fold. Although the family has many functions, public interest in it is above all centered on children—on the family's capacity to care for children and to supply what are thought to be their needs. In this context the family has for some time been prominent in the public consciousness and a subject of debate.

This essay explores the policy implications for the care of children of preprimary school age when this care and the responsibility for it are anchored in the family. In presenting a *theoretical* rationale toward this end, no attempt has been made either to render a history of the development of existing programs or to analyze such programs. The emerging policy proposals presented here are based upon the premise that the family as well as small children are in need of attention and assistance. A definition of what precisely are the "needs" of small children is beyond the limits of this discussion, which sees the family as the chief agent for the care of its own small children.

The Changing Concept of the Family

For close to a hundred years the family has been considered to be in a state of crisis, and more recently its demise has been predicted to be

1

imminent. Many academicians and policy makers have felt that the family was no longer able—indeed, in the opinion of some, no longer suited—to care for its own children. Hence they have urged that viable alternatives be developed and instituted.

Impelled by activist impulses, a rousing call for national action to save our children swept the land. Outside intervention was seen as imperative either to supplement the family's capacity to care for its children or to replace the family in that function. In any case, intervention was the chief strategy, and intervention was spearheaded by ever more professionals and financed (often lavishly) from public coffers. Today a vast child care industry has become firmly established, ever more expansionistic and ever more in need of astronomical funds.

In the face of this concerted effort, it is necessary to ask whether the family can regain its significance in the care of children. I think there is hope because the family has defied all predictions of its decline if not demise, and there is a new willingness to discuss the family in terms of its role in child care. From the perspective of mediating structures, certainly, the family is the *only* institution around that has the capacity to really take care of children. No other institution can replace it—at least not in the overwhelming majority of cases. The policy question is then how to empower the family—more accurately, how to empower innumerable particular families—to continue this crucial societal function.

In order to establish the family's viability as the chief institution of child care it will be necessary to examine the conceptualization of the family that has so widely discredited its capacity to rear and socialize children of preschool age.

The conceptualization that has significantly informed public opinion and immensely influenced policy decisions is that of American sociology. The sociological approach has been particularly useful in the formulation of social policy in past decades because it seemed possible to glean emerging trends from empirical data and subject them to sociological analysis. It was hoped that responsible policy planners could extrapolate from shifts between past and present social practices and identify trends that would require policy consideration in the future. Within sociology the dominant conceptualization combined the Chicago school view of the disintegrating effect of urbanism on traditional institutions with the structural-functional view of the Parsonian school.[1]

---

[1] The term "Chicago school" has been used to designate a whole group of sociologists working at the University of Chicago during the 1920s and 1930s. Their major interest was in the impact of the three great forces of modern American society upon individual life: urbanization, industrialization, and immigration. On

(The latter was flexible enough to accommodate some of the psycho-analytical views of Freud as well as some of the perspectives of cultural anthropology.)

The argument runs roughly as follows: The American family has been subjected to far-reaching social changes from without as well as from within. Most of the external forces are deeply rooted in the modernization processes that have transformed all important sectors of contemporary society. An ever-increasing institutional differentiation has stripped the family of its earlier functions such as education; the technologization and bureaucratization of the economy has removed the family from economic production, thus robbing it of its traditional integrative basis; urbanization—the apogee of the modernizing process —has immense consequences for the patterns of human habitation and interaction, such as the loss of kinship ties and the rise of the "conjugal nuclear" family. These external forces have a devastating effect upon the family. They were instrumental in eroding traditional sources of authority and what has been generally called the "organic bonds of solidarity" as anchored in cultural and religious traditions. The process, it was argued, in particular with the Chicago model, became most dramatically visible among immigrant and migrant families subjected to the forces of modernity.

In the process of structural and functional differentiation charac-teristic of modernization, the traditional functions of the family in rela-tion to its children were transferred to outside agencies that arose as

---

the basis of a great amount of empirically collected data in many areas of life the Chicago sociologists, in general, concurred that traditional patterns of life (or "interaction") tended to become "disorganized" and even break down under the onslaught of these novel forces making for a "transfer of functions" in a variety of ways. The publications in this tradition of sociology that influenced the perception of a family in disarray and in need of intervention are too numerous to list. For a start the reader might like to look at J. K. Folsom, *The Family: Its Sociology and Social Psychiatry* (Norwood, Penn.: Norwood Editions, 1934); Ernest Mowrer, *The Family: Its Organization and Disorganization* (Chicago: Uni-versity of Chicago Press, 1934); and Ernest Burgess and Harvey J. Locke, *The Family: From Traditional to Companionship* (1945; 4th ed., New York: Van Nostrand, 1971).

Structural-functionalism itself is a complete body of thought. The basic as-sumption that unifies the various exponents of this theoretical appraisal is that society is organized to assure its continuity and stability. The "parts" making up society may be thought of as institutions, such as the family or the school; social roles, such as mother, father, child, sister, manager; and the customs permeating both. Just like society, the family is understood to be a social system with its own institutional machine, social roles, and customs. And just like society, the family is assumed to adapt to change. The voluminous book by Talcott Parsons, Robert F. Bales, and others, *Family, Socialization, and Interaction Process* (New York: Free Press, 1955), has generally been regarded as the most influential formulation of this position with reference to the family.

more efficient and at the same time more equitable family substitutes. Thus the family was relieved of its educative, economic, and even protective functions. Simultaneously, the notion of individual rights gained credence. In sum, while the family lost many traditional functions, it gained new ones—for the individual. These new functions were celebrated by scholars standing with the final liberation of the family from outside forces. In this manner the family came to be conceived primarily in terms of emotional functions for adults and children alike. Family life now, it was emphasized, turned around mutual affection, emotional interdependence, sympathetic understanding, and similarly benign sentiments.

This sociological model of the family, which was to dominate public thinking for nearly fifty years, reflects the dichotomization between the public and the private sphere. The public sphere, primarily the economic and political institutions, was seen as a harsh, inflexible reality. The private sphere, on the other hand, mainly organized around family life, was seen as providing a "haven in a heartless world" (to use the catchy title of Christopher Lasch's recent book).[2] It was to give sustenance and emotional solace to individuals. The rearing and socialization of children in this view became an ancillary question, almost an afterthought. The increasing specialization of functions was considered beneficial since, according to Parsons, it always increases efficiency. As a result, child-rearing, too, became a professional task— indeed, Parsons's term "professionalization of parenthood" came into use.

This theoretical conceptualization of the contemporary American family is highly problematic, and aside from the important question of its empirical validity, it is filled with many practical pitfalls. With regard to the rearing and care of young children it had disastrous consequences for the family. It is exceedingly important to understand why.

The "professionalization of parenthood" opened up a veritable Pandora's box, for parents tended to be judged by their ability to approximate whatever the current professional standards of child-rearing demanded and whatever the latest orthodoxy prescribed. At this point the problems of the family multiplied like an amoeba, and the family could indeed be found wanting. What characterizes the family that is successful in the primary socialization of its children? Answering this question became a major preoccupation, particularly among the phenomenally increasing number of psychologists. Studies and literature began to pile up, and astounding amounts of time and energy were

---

[2] Christopher Lasch, *Haven in a Heartless World: The Family Besieged* (New York: Basic Books, 1977).

spent in identifying the "good home." Family size was judged to be a determinant, and small families became a national goal, with huge programs and agencies dedicated to family planning. For a long time the "disastrous effect upon the child of an unstable home situation"[3] stirred the nation, as ever more homes were found to be unstable, broken, or in the process of breaking up. There were endless debates about what precisely constitutes a "stable home" and supposedly makes it beneficial: Must it have both a father and a mother? Could an effective mother be working outside the home? Should mothers look upon child-rearing as a career? And what should fathers be like—nonauthoritarian, hard working, yet also ever present and available as companions to their children? Or, as others claimed, does the affectionate, child-centered mother in the final analysis deprive her children of the opportunity to develop into autonomous individuals? And, of course, does this definition of the mother role deprive women of their own opportunities to grow as human beings? As to the father, is the authoritarian, demanding, aloof, and much-absent type really so bad for his children?

As was to be expected, there were no clear-cut answers to any of these questions. Controversies proliferated, as did efforts to specify and measure favorable "parental attitudes"—favorable, that is, to parents performing well in their "professionalized" roles. From a scientific point of view, these measures were mainly crude and unsophisticated; what is more, it was far from clear just what was being measured. The available data suggest extreme caution before one identifies "effective" parenting with kindly and understanding attitudes. Insofar as "effectiveness" has to do with educational achievement of children, there are data indicating that good students often come from demanding, rigid, unreasoning, even ruthless homes.[4]

In any case, all these scholarly efforts to determine what is a "good" family have not led to a coherent and unambiguous concept. Fuzzy studies, dubious theories, competing and contradictory intellectual orthodoxies make for a veritable morass of notions surrounding the family. Nor were these ambiguous findings and contradictory claims of any help to the middle-class and literate parents who wanted to approximate the professionalized model for the benefit of their children. As they strove to keep themselves informed of the latest "scientific" insights on child-rearing, they became increasingly uncertain of their own child-rearing capacity—the more so since in most cases the expert advice did not lead to the desired results. These parents became disoriented

---

[3] M. E. Nimkoff, *The Family* (Boston: Houghton Mifflin, 1934), pp. 374–375.

[4] Frank Musgrove, *The Family, Education and Society* (London: Routledge & Kegan Paul, 1966), has an excellent summary of the "good home" argument.

and ultimately so discouraged that they gave up. They began to abdicate the rearing of their children to outside professional agencies, and whatever child-rearing was done in the middle-class home had to be done on the advice and under the supervision of experts. A vague sense of guilt remained that was strong enough to make middle-class parents accept the enormous financial costs that arose from their abdication. When a new definition of womanhood emerged under the influence of the women's movement and a variety of other forces that became strongly effective by the 1960s, middle-class women started to leave the home in ever larger numbers to enter the world of work—a trend that was to have a profound effect upon child care policy. The needs of children were seen to be independent from the home. At this point the middle-class family completed the abdication of its child-caring role in favor of the child care industry.

If the professionalization of parenthood has created disarray in middle-class families, its influence on the non-middle-class segment of the population has been devastating. The differentiated effects of this model according to class cannot be emphasized enough. It is still possible for strong middle-class parents to survive the onslaught against the family—at least they have the financial means, the verbal skills, and the bureaucratic knowledge to navigate around the most blatantly obvious dangers to themselves and their children. The poorer classes, however, lack the protection of money, status, and verbal know-how and thus are particularly vulnerable in this situation. More than anyone else, they become the powerless victims of "friendly intruders," as they and their children come under the tutelage of experts, agencies, and institutions, who begin to run their lives for them. It is not much of a consolation to be reminded that these institutions and organizations were originally designed to aid the poor and their children. The realities that have emerged stand in stark contrast to the benevolent rhetoric underpinning the efforts made on their behalf. Sheila Rothman in a recent essay has succinctly analyzed the situation of poor families when middle-class values inspire government intervention in their affairs under the slogan of improving the quality of life.[5] Instead of aiding poor families to cope and succeed, instead of liberating them and enhancing their individual choices, frequently this intervention has exactly the opposite result. More coercion and greater loss of choice and individual freedom loom on the horizon of poor parents who have

---

[5] Sheila Rothman, "Rights v. Needs: American Attitudes toward Women, Children and the Family," in Irving Kristol and Paul H. Weaver, eds., *The Americans: 1976*, Critical Choices for Americans Series, vol. 2 (Lexington, Mass.: Lexington Books, 1976).

become pawns in the grubby power game of experts and bureaucrats. The effect upon the black family has been particularly disastrous. It is this tutelage of the poor that leaders like Jesse Jackson are seeking to break through.

These paradoxical effects certainly were not intended by the scholars who formulated the sociological model of the modern family. And in the 1950s the "professionalization of parenthood" conceptualization probably had some empirical grounding in the life of middle-class America. The major problem, however, rarely discussed at that time, was that policy makers and child care bureaucrats took over the model without question to measure and judge non-middle-class families. As a rule, the problems of poor and lower-class families were understood to stem largely from their "adult-centered" (that is, *not* "child-centered") style of life, as well as from their ignorance of the enlightened child-rearing practices middle-class families emphasized under the tutelage of child care experts. Slowly, under immense pressures, the lower classes began to respond, and poor women became desirous of staying home to care for their children and to dedicate themselves to their many needs. In other words, they aspired to the criteria of "professionalized parenthood" with whatever modest means they had, and becoming child-centered was one of the few means they had at their disposal. But by the time these changes were under way, the concept was already outmoded and no longer functional. The realization that the concept was not applicable had permeated the middle classes, and with them the policy-making sector as well as the child care bureaucracy run by middle-class people. The conceptualization of the needs of children in relation to their families had shifted by 180 degrees.

In the words of Sheila Rothman, "while in previous decades the foremost problem was *how* to induce individual members of the family to live up to their obligations and make the family thereby more effective, the issue today is *not how* but *whether* to strengthen the family."[6] Again under the influence of political pressure groups from the middle classes, whose priorities had changed fundamentally, new needs for children were discovered and demands for new kinds of services were urgently vocalized. Once more the poor were lagging behind. The specific cultural milieus of lower-class and ethnic-racial familism were found to be suspect and, in fact, were judged to be a major problem. By the early 1970s many observers viewed the family as a lost enterprise, not only for the middle class, but for all other classes as well.

As a result of changing attitudes, alternatives to the family were

---

[6] Sheila Rothman, "Rights v. Needs."

sought that could take over more effectively and more humanely the functions of the family—this time among all social classes. Combines of psychologists, educationists, sociologists, social workers, child care specialists, child care bureaucrats, and the like vigorously set out to develop such alternatives. But since there were no clear conceptualizations, no coherent policies could follow. The old familiar paradoxes from the "good home" debate continued and multiplied. While one set of experts tended to propagate the continuation of a family-like setting as the breeding ground of personality development and individuation, another set perceived the very same setting as a threat to this development and to the rise of strong selves. Frequently the same professionals who popularized the importance of intimate groups for personality development stood ready to intervene through increased state control and laws to break up the existing intimate environment. At all times, of course, any of the positions or actions taken increased the influence, control, and number of jobs for the same professional groups. The aggressive imperialism of the child and family coalitions is a frightening spectacle to behold. The leviathan empire of the educationists may perhaps claim the debatable honor of holding the lion's share of the influence and jobs in the past decade. In any case, by the mid-1970s it seemed as if the battle for the family were lost.

The Reaffirmation of the Family's Role in Child-Rearing

However, the vagaries of the family–child care debate are wondrous indeed. Today, after more than fifty years of viewing the family as facing an acute crisis, after more than a decade of the most vigorous attacks on the family, after frantic and sometimes even bizarre searches for alternatives, and precisely at a time when a reform-oriented child care bureaucracy was firmly established at last, the tide has turned again. This shift has to be seen within a wider context. In the wake of a general disenchantment with the rather dismal results, the exorbitant costs, and the unanticipated consequences of the many reform-oriented attempts and intervention programs growing out of the Great Society strategy of the 1960s, we seem to be entering what has been called a postreformist era. Naturally, the family too, if not above all, tends to be reevaluated in light of this rapidly spreading and contagious post-reformist mood. To the surprise of some and the delight of others, it has become fashionable again to speak of the family as the chief agent in the rearing and socialization of the younger child.

This turn of events does not mean that liberal reform-oriented professionals and administrators do not firmly control the child care bureaucracy, nor that public sentiment and commitment to the welfare of the nation's children has faltered. The change has come about in part because of the poor performance of many alternative programs; the persistence and even multiplication, if not magnification, of targeted problems in spite of (or because of, as some would claim) massive intervention and immense sums spent from public coffers; the shocking realization that enlightened recommendations and well-intentioned programs frequently have led to "mental totalitarianism" as well as the astounding expansion of the discretionary authority of professional complexes; and the grass-roots reaction against a pervasive tutelage and "dependency" of whole population groups. In the words of David Rothman, "the commitment to paternalistic state intervention in the name of equality is giving way to a commitment to restrict intervention in the name of liberty."[7] All these factors have combined to change the public mood. But the most important factor, which tends to be ignored, has been the unrealistic conceptualization of the family and of the needs of children. The new perception of the family as a mediating structure may help to provide a new conceptualization.

Very relevant to the conceptualization of the continuing central function of the family in the rearing and socialization of children is research such as that of Mary Jo Bane and her associates on the staying power of the contemporary American family, published under the title *Here to Stay*.[8] This and other newly available data on the contemporary as well as the traditional family cast serious doubt on many of the clichés that have for some time been used as evidence of the demise of the family and that have informed child care policies. Today there is empirical justification for emphasizing the staying power and the strength of the family instead of belaboring its erosion and weakness.

Since the family is obviously here to stay, the most informed in the child care debate have recently shifted gears and now tend to identify the task as that of determining the needs and problems of the family. The goal is to aid the family and to remove the obstacles that seem to interfere with the family's most recently rediscovered function, the care of children. Above all, there has been vigorous agitation toward a national family policy. The screws are being put on the politicians, who, as is the way with politicians, are likely to respond by compromise and accommodation to the most loudly vocal groups. Clearly, the family is a hot issue again. The question, however, is, *Will the family survive its new champions?*

---

[7] David Rothman, in W. Gaylin and others, *Doing Good: The Limits of Benevolence* (New York: Pantheon, 1978).

[8] Mary Jo Bane, *Here to Stay: American Families in the Twentieth Century* (New York: Basic Books, 1976).

I do not ask this lightly. In this new postreformist stance there is a danger that we may simply be presented with a new rhetoric of social policy. It may be that down in the bowels of the institutional world, the changes may not be so dramatic. But more than that, there seems to be a de facto continuation of the previous trend, this time, however, disguised as an appeal to populist sentiments. A close examination of the most recent proposals of the new champions of the family (such as Kenneth Keniston and the Carnegie Council on Children[9]) makes clear that old utopianisms do not die easily. Thus, while it is no longer said that paradise would be gained by replacing the family, it is now implicitly suggested that the family should become the tool for changing society. It is difficult to say which position is worse. Those who once thought too little of the family, even to the point of wanting to destroy it, now think too much of it. The family is envisioned as a vehicle for the redistribution of income, for tax reform, for a full employment policy. At the same time it is to be enlisted in the struggles against environmental pollution and depletion, against the omnipresent power of multinational corporations, and against the interference of big business in the proper domain of the media. Once more the children and their families tend to be reduced to pawns in a power game, and the issues are essentially political. As a result the battle for the family seems to be merely symbolic.

If it is true that the family is the only viable institution for child-rearing, and we indeed wish to return the care of children to the family, some pressing questions must be addressed: Are the ways ordinary families care for their children defensible? Are there any clear-cut findings on "superior" and "inferior" cultural styles affecting children? Are different styles of bringing up children equally beneficial to children's socialization—or at least tolerable? To put the question a better way, with the knowledge of the impact of alternative experiments, can different styles of child-rearing be defended? What is "deprivation" and to what degree does state intervention change the intolerable situation of deprivation?

If, however, we intend to use the family as an instrument for more complex changes, the programs sponsored by the new champions of the family will probably experience the same fate as the top priority recommendations of the 1970 White House Conference on Children.[10] Called "modest proposals," the first three recommendations were:

---

[9] Kenneth Keniston and the Carnegie Council on Children, *All Our Children: The American Family under Pressure* (New York: Harcourt Brace, 1977).

[10] *White House Conference on Children* (Washington, D.C.: Government Printing Office, 1970).

- Comprehensive family-oriented child-development programs including health services, day care, and early childhood education. The proposal of a national day care program resulted directly from this.
- Development of a program to eliminate the racism that cripples all children. Court-enforced busing was seen to be the answer here.
- Reordering of national priorities, beginning with a guaranteed basic family income adequate for the needs of children. This was at a time when the Nixon Family Assistance Plan, called by some "a guaranteed annual income," was dropped from the political stage.

Two years after the White House conference, under pressure from conservative groups, President Nixon vetoed a bill calling for day care, and in spite of the wide publicity given to the Brademas-Mondale proposal for a national day care program in 1976, the proposal has been shelved. The busing of school children has emerged as a greater concern among large segments of the population (including blacks) than the persistence of the racism it is supposed to counteract. And the bill for a guaranteed annual income, a revolutionary concept put forth by a conservative president, died in Congress. Why was that so? In the words of one observer, "It seemed clear that the mood of the country was against such a proposal at that time."[11] In spite of the widely recognized and urgent needs of children, in spite of the awareness of the crippling consequences of an intolerable racism, in spite of widespread dissatisfaction with the present welfare system and the way it is administered, the American public remained suspicious of these proposals—and for very good reasons. The proposals seemed to hold very little promise of solving the problems they were supposed to tackle. For ordinary American citizens, a national day care program would entail mammoth costs and additional tax burdens, and, perhaps more important, the program itself implied a further devalidation of the family and its power over its children. Enforced busing, aside from being of dubious effect, added to racial strife instead of combating it; moreover, there is an understandable reluctance to use children, the weakest segment of society, to conduct the large and haunting battle over racism. And a guaranteed income, at least as proposed at that time, seemed not fit to fight the existing poverty. Aside from their symbolic value, such proposals implied the continuation of the major trend of the twentieth century: the assertion of social control over activities once left to individuals, and the expropriation of ever wider areas of life by the modern state.

---

[11] Arlene Skolnick, *The Intimate Environment: Exploring Marriage and the Family* (Boston: Little Brown, 1973), p. 440.

The basic flaw in these attempts was that all too often analysts and social reformers, however committed and sincere, relied on their own observations and inclinations instead of on those of the public they claimed to benefit. In taking seriously ordinary people's understanding of life, in respecting their values, hopes, and life styles, and in giving credence to the institutions that continue to play the major role in structuring their everyday life, the mediating-structures approach may help to avoid the arrogance and the patronizing tone that has characterized many of the widely acclaimed policy proposals of late.

As the major institution in the life of individuals, the family, more than ever before, is for most people in our society the most valuable thing in their lives. It is around the family that individuals continue to make moral commitments, to invest emotions and hope, and to plan for the future. The high divorce rates, which are usually cited as proof of the decline of the family, probably indicate the very opposite: It is because marriage and family are valued so highly that individuals want to get out of situations that seem not to meet these high expectations. The high remarriage rate may serve to support this interpretation. Furthermore, even radical challenges to the nuclear bourgeois family do not envisage destroying the institution but reconstructing it in accordance with different desiderata to form communal families, group families, homosexual families, or auxiliary families. Whatever the criteria may be, for most Americans some version of the much maligned bourgeois family, however modified, continues to be both the norm and the social reality of their lives. There is no reason to think that this is about to change fundamentally.

A National Family Policy

I believe that there ought to be public recognition of the family as an institution, particularly in the area of child-rearing, and a public commitment to further and support this institution, instead of continuing efforts to dismantle it. I am somewhat doubtful about the expediency of a national family plan, however. American society is much too pluralistic. The coexistence of diverse groups of varying cultural origins and the preservation of intentional communities of the widest variety are much too important to make a standardized national family plan easily feasible. I agree with the many people who say it is wrong to assume that all families function with two parents—a working father, a homemaking mother, and dependent children. I would be reluctant to have the presumed needs of any particular group generalized to the rest of society and codified in governmentally enforced programs. There are too many different groups, embedded in too many different structures, with widely varying perceptions, goals, and values. They imply that it may not be desirable to deal with most problems of the American family through governmentally devised and implemented programs in the form of a "well-concerted social strategy." The dismal record of past programs hardly encourages optimism that future performance would be much better.

I am *not* taking a right-wing position opposing *all* government action on these problems. Caution need not mean inaction. There are pressing social forces that make government action on family problems, including child care, very likely and perhaps desirable. All the more urgent is the question of what kind of action this will be. If there is to be a national family policy, it should not be conceived as a panacea for all problems of society. The policy should recognize the family as the primary institution of child care and at the same time be responsive to different needs. Above all, this policy should guarantee the greatest amount of freedom and choice.

A national family policy should be guided, in my opinion, by the following ideas:

1. *The family—and no other conceivable structure—is the most viable locale for child care.* In defiance of the monopoly of often self-styled experts of child care and engineers of family welfare, the emphasis should again be on individual families themselves. Despite a history of ambivalence and distrust of parents, in particular those who are poor and members of minority groups, parents should again be seen as the best advocates of their children's welfare.

Relying upon parents once more, however, does not imply a restrictive definition of the family. Anyone who is willing to commit himself or herself to the care of a child for a number of years is to be included in this category. It should be accepted that a great variety of people, with the most varied styles of life, can be effective parents, as long as they meet the above conditions. Single-headed households, lesbians and homosexuals, older individuals or couples, and others who do not meet the traditional narrow definitions have to be included in the parental category.

2. *Insofar as professional services and agencies have to be involved in the process of child care, they should be ancillary to the family and as far as possible be held accountable to parents.* The best way to assure accountability, in my opinion, is to make available to parents some kind of voucher that is used at their discretion to secure professional services. The intention here is by no means to denigrate the professional as such, but to attempt to clarify the professional's role in relation to the

family. There does exist a real need for professional advice and services, and by far the great majority of child care professionals have the best interest of the child at heart. If, however, the child is best served within the family (as widely defined above), then it follows that professional services are to be ancillary to the family.

3. *A national family policy should respect the existing pluralism of family life styles and child care practices.* This implies that the particular pattern of any given group—including the typical middle class as well as the poor and ethnic minorities—is neither belittled nor elevated. This also means that a national family policy should not be guided by any given middle-class standards and needs, nor by the needs of targeted groups, such as female-headed poor ethnic households, as those needs are currently understood.

To assure in practice, and not only in rhetoric, respect for the great variety of American life styles, for their widely varying perceptions and goals, as well as for the distinctive structures in which they are embedded, and yet to be responsive to the different needs of families and their children, some sort of child-allowance seems to be indicated. This mechanism, in my opinion, would resolve most of the controversies around the national day care debate. A child-allowance would allow individual families the widest possible choice in arranging for the care of their small children. The varied forms of care should including the option for the individual parent (father or mother) to stay home during the crucial period of infancy and early childhood (or longer (as well as arrangements such as "grandparenting," care by extended-family members or neighborhood groups, child care centers attached to the place of work, part-time, full-time, even hourly arrangements at drop-in centers, as well as existing and to-be-established governmental centers of any size.

4. *Any national family policy has to free itself from the pejorative myths that surround the black family.* There has been a widespread tendency to view and treat the black family, especially the poor black family, as "disorganized," "broken," and even "pathological." But recent research, such as that of Robert Hill,[12] has found a vitality, a stability, and, what is more, a flexibility among black cooperative and kinship networks in rural areas as well as in cities that have been ignored heretofore. These studies suggest that black families have persisted despite poverty primarily through tight kinship bonds and mutual aid. National policy should recognize and support such bonds, not only among blacks but among other minorities as well.

---

[12] Robert B. Hill, *Strengths of Black Families* (New York: Emerson Hall Publications, 1973).

Wherever kinship networks do break down, local neighborhood substitutes for the family, such as the House of Umoja in Philadelphia, which emerged within the community on a voluntaristic basis, should be recognized and supported.[13]

5. *The thesis of the primacy of the family should apply to the various categories of "special children" as well.* To counter the trend to separate the handicapped from their own families, the family should be understood as the most stable structure available for meeting some of the primary needs of special children. Where the family is not able to care for its special children, they should be placed in settings as close to a family situation as possible. Professional staffs and services should be looked upon as back-up supports for families rather than as substitutes for them.

This approach may include paying special child-allowances to families who care for their own handicapped children so that family members can work less or not at all outside the home in order to meet the extraordinary needs of their children, or so that they can employ help that is accountable to them. One advantage—but by no means the most important one—is that this approach would almost certainly reduce costs to the state.

6. *A national family policy must not become an instrument for further weakening the family by emphasizing children's rights to the detriment of the rights of their parents.*

Family rights should be emphasized more than children's rights in spite of the current preoccupation with child abuse. This emphasis seems to be justified by data such as those presented by Rena Uviller of the American Civil Liberties Union.[14] In spite of tragic cases of true physical abuse (approximately 4 percent of the hundreds of thousands annually reported), the more than 450,000 children who are separated from their parents each year (150,000 are taken coercively and about 300,000 are yielded to state custody "voluntarily" by their parents under threat of prosecution for neglect) have rarely fared well. Separation from their families means for them an endless stream of foster homes, confusion, and heartache, frequently resulting in irreparable psychological damage. A most stringent application of existing laws is called for in those tragic cases that do occur. In most cases, however, such "crimes" as parental immaturity, sloppy housekeeping, or "failure to provide for the moral and emotional welfare of a child" hardly seem to justify breaking up a family.

---

[13] House of Umoja is reported by Robert Woodson in a forthcoming book in the Mediating Structures Project of the American Enterprise Institute.

[14] Rena Uviller, *New York Times*, April 20, 1977, op.ed. page.

7. *In the context of the emerging debate on income support and income redistribution, a national family policy should be guided by the general principle that reforms intended to diminish poverty defeat their own purpose if they weaken the family.*

2
Child Care Settings in the United States

Mary Jo Bane, Laura Lein, Lydia O'Donnell,
C. Ann Stueve, and Barbara Welles

Over the last decade or so, child care has become an important topic of public debate. The debate has been spurred partly by fear that increasing labor force participation by mothers means that children are being neglected. There have been claims and counterclaims about the effects of day care centers and discussion about whether government should provide more or fewer day care facilities for children of working mothers.

It seems to be assumed that mothers' participation in the labor force necessarily requires substantial out-of-home care for children, that day care centers and family day care homes are the major institutions that are replacing parents in caring for children, and that government support for day care would signal a dramatic change in the ways children are taken care of.

This paper argues that those assumptions are not true and that the debate about child care policy has been conducted in fundamentally misleading terms. If the narrow concept of child care is broadened to include the institutions that in fact care for children under age fourteen, it is evident that the most important caretakers of children, now as in the past, are nuclear families and public schools. They are supplemented by a rich and diverse array of extended family, community, and market arrangements that answer to families' differing needs and preferences. Labor force participation by mothers makes some difference in how families manage child care, but not as much as is sometimes assumed.

Child care is an important responsibility and a costly proposition. Because this society has long recognized that children are national resources for the future as well as members of families, the cost of caring

NOTE: Part of the analysis and preparation for this paper was funded by the Robert Sterling Clark Foundation.

17

for children is therefore shared between parents and the society as a whole. The policy question is not, therefore, whether government should begin to "interfere" in child-rearing, but whether government should extend or change its participation. The mechanisms by which government shares the cost of child care can have important effects on the range and diversity of institutions available, depending on whether it encourages nuclear families, public schools, or the development of supplementary institutions. This poses perhaps the most important question for child care policy over the next decade.

When child care and child care policy are seen in the broader framework proposed here, the issues become less stark and frightening. They remain issues, to be sure, of the level of government cost-sharing, of the balance between families and schools, and of the variety and choice in arrangements that supplement parents and public schools. We do not settle these questions in this paper, but we do hope to influence the terms in which they are asked.

The Institutions of Child Care

The major institutions caring for children under age fourteen in the United States are nuclear families and public schools. The balance of time and responsibility for children shifts between the two institutions as children grow older. The extent to which other arrangements supplement families and schools also changes as children age. Within age groups, arrangements for children reflect a variety of family circumstances, including the work commitments of the parents and, perhaps more importantly, their notions of appropriate settings for children.

In describing the current American patterns of child care arrangements we make use of both published national survey data and intensive studies of families conducted by the authors. The data and their limitations are described in the appendix.

Nuclear Families. Nuclear families appear to be the major caretakers of young children aged three to thirteen, despite the current high proportions of mothers in the labor force. Table 2–1, calculated from the 1975 National Child Care Consumer Study (NCCCS), shows the proportion of children who spend various amounts of time in nonparental, nonschool child care arrangements. Because some children are cared for by a combination of methods, proportions cannot, strictly speaking, be added up across child care modes. It is clear from the table, nonetheless, that a maximum of 13 percent of children aged two or younger spend thirty hours per week or more in nonparental care. In fact, only a high maximum (because of duplicated counts) of 28 percent of

18

TABLE 2–1

PERCENTAGE OF CHILDREN USING NONPARENTAL CARE,
BY AGE AND MODE

Age and Hours per Week	In Home by Relative	In Home Non-relative	Rela-tive's Home	Nonrela-tive's Home	Nursery	Day Care
Two years or less						
9 hours or less	25	23	27	14	1	1
10–29 hours	3	3	4	3	1	1
30 hours or more	3	1	3	4	1	1
Total	31	27	34	21	3	3
Three to five years						
9 hours or less	23	26	29	15	7	1
10–29 hours	3	3	4	3	4	1
30 hours or more	2	1	3	4	3	3
Total	28	30	36	22	14	5
Six to thirteen years						
9 hours or less	15	15	15	11	1	1
10–29 hours	2	2	3	2	1	1
30 hours or more	2	1	2	1	1	1
Total	19	18	20	14	3	3

NOTE: The table does not distinguish children who were cared for by more than one mode.

SOURCE: Thomas Ward Rodes and John C. Moore, *National Child Care Consumer Study* (Arlington, Va.: Unco, Inc., 1975), vol. 2, tables IV-6–IV-11; Base number of children for calculating percentages from vol. 1, table IV-28.

children aged two years or less spend even ten hours per week in non-parental care—this despite the fact that 35 percent of mothers of children under three were participants in the paid labor force.[1]

The importance of parental care for children aged three to thirteen is less easily discernible from the table since, as will be documented later, large proportions of these children are in school. However, 1974 and 1975 Census Bureau surveys, which asked parents "Who cares for (the child) during the day when (he or she) is not in school?" suggest the continued importance of parental care.[2] Tables 2–2 and 2–3 show

[1] Howard Hayghe, "Marital and Family Characteristics of Workers, March 1977," *Monthly Labor Review*, February 1978, pp. 51–54.

[2] U.S. Bureau of the Census, "Daytime Care of Children: October 1974 and February 1975," *Current Population Reports*, Series P-20, no. 298 (Washington, D.C.: 1976).

TABLE 2–2

PERCENTAGE OF THREE-TO-SIX-YEAR-OLDS CARED FOR DURING THE
DAY BY PARENTS, BY RACE AND LABOR FORCE STATUS OF MOTHER,
FEBRUARY 1975

Race and Labor Force Status of Mother	Percent of Children[a]	Percent Cared for by		
		Mother	Father	Parents
White				
Full-time	19.7	33.2	7.1	40.3
Part-time	13.3	73.3	3.6	76.9
Not working	66.9	96.0	0.4	96.4
Total	100.0			82.5
Black				
Full-time	30.3	32.1	12.4	44.5
Part-time	11.1	52.7	10.5	63.2
Not working	58.7	88.5	0.3	88.8
Total	100.0			72.4

[a] Percentages may not add to 100 because of rounding.

SOURCE: U.S. Bureau of the Census, "Daytime Care of Children: October 1974 and February 1975," *Current Population Reports*, Series P-20, no. 298 (Washington, D.C., 1976).

the percentage of children whose parents reported themselves as the main caretaker by age, race, and labor force status of the mother. Over 80 percent of both three-to-six-year-old and seven-to-thirteen-year-old children are cared for mainly by parents. Even among those with full-time working mothers, over 40 percent of three-to-five-year-olds and over half of six-to-thirteen-year-olds are cared for by parents.

How do they do it? Many use school and other arrangements for short periods to help out. In addition, some husbands and wives arrange their work hours at different times so that one parent is available to take care of the children most of the time. The Working Family Project, a study of lower-middle-income two-worker families with preschoolers in the Boston area, found that one-third of the families staggered parental work hours.[3] With either a part-time work schedule or staggered

[3] Working Family Project, Preliminary Report, *Work and Family Life* (Washington, D.C.: National Institute of Mental Health and National Institute of Education, 1974).

TABLE 2–3

PERCENTAGE OF SEVEN-TO-THIRTEEN-YEAR-OLDS CARED FOR DURING
THE DAY BY PARENTS, BY RACE AND LABOR FORCE STATUS OF MOTHER,
OCTOBER 1974

Race and Labor Force Status of Mother	Percent of Children[a]	Percent Cared for by Parents
White		
Full-time	26.7	54.7
Part-time	15.6	84.6
Not working	57.7	93.7
Total	100.0	81.4
Black		
Full-time	34.7	49.3
Part-time	11.9	75.2
Not working	53.4	90.9
Total	100.0	74.5

[a] Percentages may not add to 100 because of rounding.
SOURCE: U.S. Bureau of the Census, "Daytime Care of Children: October 1974 and February 1975," *Current Population Reports*, Series P-20, no. 298 (Washington, D.C., 1976).

hours, relatively small amounts of nonparental care can complete the families' child care packages.

A few case studies from the Working Family Project can give a flavor of how these arrangements work for Boston families with three-to-five-year-olds:

The Henrys: Mr. Henry works at building maintenance, a job that is usually 8:00 A.M.–4:00 P.M. except for two evenings a week when he is on call to work through the evening until about 8:00 P.M. Mrs. Henry works in a factory on a 4:00–11:00 P.M. shift. However, both Mr. and Mrs. Henry need to commute about half an hour to their jobs. Because of commuting time, there is an hour in the day between 3:30, when Mrs. Henry must leave for work, and 4:30, when Mr. Henry returns, that must be covered in other ways; in addition, there are occasional evenings to be covered when Mr. Henry works overtime. In order to cover these hours, the Henrys exchange child care with one of the neighbors. Mr. and Mrs. Henry are likely to return this favor by participating in baby-sitting over

21

the weekends or having children with them when one or the other is home from work.

The Hunts: The Hunt family is reluctant to consider day care or nursery school as a mechanism for allowing both adults to work at the same time, even though their children do attend child care programs outside the home. Their youngest son Henry goes to a day care center one morning each week because he seems to enjoy it *and* because his grandmother operates the center. The Hunts pay a fee for this service. Their older son John attends local public kindergarten every morning. John and Henry are sent to outside child care for the opportunity to be with other children, that is, for socializing experiences, not for employment considerations. Mr. and Mrs. Hunt work completely different schedules. Mr. Hunt, a supervisor in a large company, works a 9:00–5:00 schedule, while Mrs. Hunt works a 3:00–11:00 shift as a key punch operator. Their two children are cared for by a baby sitter only from 3:00–5:00 every day. Otherwise, the Hunt children are continuously in the care of one parent or the other.

The Dens: One option for many families—which is not necessarily clear from the national statistics—is for mothers to become paid day care providers during their own children's preschool years. Mr. and Mrs. Den, for instance, have one child, Camille. Mrs. Den was determined to stay home with her daughter while Mr. Den continued his work as a nurse. However, in part because she enjoyed children, and in part to supplement the family income, Mrs. Den became a family day care provider. Mrs. Den takes her job very seriously. She has taken courses in early childhood education and has collected a large selection of appropriate play materials. She enjoys analyzing and dealing carefully with each child's problems and achievements. However, when their own daughter reached the age of three, Mr. and Mrs. Den agreed that Camille needed some time away from home and her mother. Thus, at the time the Dens were interviewed, Camille attended nursery school daily from 9:00–12:00 while her mother remained at home, providing child care for others.[4]

Why do families make these complicated, demanding care arrangements? Working Family Project respondents report caring deeply about the importance of parental care for young children. Almost all feel that parents are best able to provide reliable, continuous, loving care;

---

[4] These cases are taken from data collected by the Working Family Project and by the Families and Communities Project; both are described in the appendix to this chapter.

TABLE 2–4

PERCENTAGE OF CHILDREN ENROLLED IN PREPRIMARY PROGRAMS,
BY AGE, 1967 AND 1976

Age	1967	1976	Percent Increase 1967–1976
Three years	6.8	20.0	194.1
Four years	21.3	41.9	96.2
Five years	65.4	81.4	24.5

SOURCE: U.S. Bureau of the Census, "Nursery School and Kindergarten Enrollment of Children and Labor Force Status of Their Mothers: October 1967 to October 1976," *Current Population Reports*, Series P-20, no. 318 (Washington, D.C., 1978), table 1.

that they are best able to protect their children from too early development or from values and standards which conflict with the parents' own.[5] In addition, of course, parental care is cheap in terms of money to be paid out. Costs in inconvenience, energy, and lack of shared time are for many less important than the benefits of parental care.

Schools. Schools have long been the most important nonparental caretakers of children over five. In recent years, kindergartens, preschools, and nursery schools have become increasingly prominent caretakers of children three to five as well. Table 2–4 shows the dramatic growth in preprimary school enrollment between 1967 and 1976. Table 2–5 shows current patterns of enrollment of three-to-thirteen-year-olds by age, race, and level of school. Nearly 100 percent of children aged six to thirteen are enrolled in school, the vast majority (about 90 percent) in public schools. In addition, 53 percent of children aged three to five were enrolled in school in 1976. For this age group, public provision of schooling is somewhat less dominant, with 31.5 percent of nursery school and kindergarten children in private schools.[6]

The Hunts, described earlier, use school as a supplement to pa-

[5] See Working Family Project, *Work and Family Life*; and Laura Lein, "Parental Evaluation of Child Care Alternatives" (Wellesley College Center for Research on Women, December 1978; processed).

[6] Data on public-private provisions of schooling are from U.S. Bureau of the Census, "School Enrollment—Social and Economic Characteristics of Students: October 1976," *Current Population Reports*, Series P-20, no. 319 (Washington, D.C., 1976).

23

TABLE 2–5

PERCENTAGE OF CHILDREN ENROLLED IN SCHOOL, BY
AGE AND RACE, 1976

Age and Race	Nursery	Kinder- garten	Elementary, Middle, and High	Total
Total population				
Three years	19	1	0	20
Four years	27	15	0	42
Five years	2	79	11	92
Six years	<1	6	92	98
Seven to thirteen years	0	0	99	99
Black				
Three years	19	2	0	21
Four years	25	22	0	47
Five years	2	79	14	95
Six years	<1	4	93	97
Seven to thirteen years	0	0	99	99
White				
Three years	18	1	0	19
Four years	27	14	0	41
Five years	2	80	10	92
Six years	<1	6	93	99
Seven to thirteen years	0	0	99	99

SOURCE: U.S. Bureau of the Census, "School Enrollment—Social and Economic Characteristics of Students: October 1976," *Current Population Reports*, Series P-20, no. 319 (Washington, D.C., 1978), table 1.

rental care. Two other families from the Working Family Project illustrate the importance of schools in putting together child care packages:

The Wyatts: Like many families, the Wyatts are multiple care users of nursery school, baby sitter, and, in emergencies, relatives. Although Mrs. Wyatt works full time during prime daytime hours, she is not using full-time day care; rather she has put together a complex child care package to meet her priorities. Mr. Wyatt is a police officer who moonlights as a mason. His wife is a full-time clerical worker at an office complex near their home. She returned to work during an extended layoff of her husband. Mrs. Wyatt rises at 5:30 A.M. in order to be at work by 8:00. Her husband gets up with her for coffee and leaves immediately afterward so that he can be at work at 7:00. Mrs. Wyatt is thus responsible for preparing Oliver for nursery school and Chris for first grade in the local elementary school. Since Mrs. Wyatt also must leave for work before the school day begins, she has made special arrangements with her neighbors to get each child off to school. Oliver is picked up by Mrs. Gray who cares for him along with her own child until both can be delivered to nursery school, for which the Wyatts pay about $1,400 a year. Chris walks to a friend's house and waits there until school time. At noon, Oliver and his young friend return to the Gray's house, where they play together until Chris comes to pick up his younger brother at 2:30. Chris and Oliver then walk to another neighbor's home where they are cared for (at a cost of $1.00 an hour) until 5:00, when their mother returns from work.

Mr. and Mrs. Wyatt spent many weeks searching for a child care facility, hoping and finally finding a program that combines the structured kind of educational program they thought would be best for Oliver with what they considered to be essential safety features. For example, in their selection process, Mr. Wyatt ruled out any day care facilities or nurseries that did not require fire drills. In addition, still needing an afternoon caretaker, Mrs. Wyatt searched for a neighborhood baby sitter and was introduced to a suitable woman by her next-door neighbor. If all goes well the Wyatt's child care package works smoothly—but it can be undone by illness or other emergencies in the Wyatt family or in the two neighborhood families who provide care to their sons. This care is reasonably expensive, since both nursery school and neighborhood baby sitters must be paid.

The Bishops: The Bishops are a younger family who have recently moved into the community with seven-year-old Jason and three-year-old Julie. Mr. Bishop is a high school history teacher during the school year, with several evening commitments as well as an all-day work schedule. In the summer months he directs a community arts and crafts program which demands that he often spend ten to twelve hours a day on the job. Mrs. Bishop has just begun a cottage industry with a friend, Mrs. Holland. They make children's toys, working six hours a day during the winter and four hours a day during the summer. Mrs. Bishop arranges her work hours to coincide with her children's school hours.

During the school year, Jason walks to school in the morning and is picked up by his mother and younger sister in the afternoon. With Jason in school, Mrs. Bishop has time to drive Julie to nursery school at 9:00 A.M. on her way to Mrs. Holland's house, where the two women work until 11:30 A.M. Mrs. Bishop then drives back to the nursery school to pick up Julie and returns to the Holland household where they eat lunch together. Julie amuses herself for the remaining hour or two while her mother finishes work and mother and daughter both leave to pick up Jason.

During the summer months these child care arrangements change. Jason sometimes accompanies his father to the community art camp, which Julie is still too young to attend. A baby sitter is hired jointly with Mrs. Holland to look after Julie and six-year-old Steve Holland, while the women work four hours each morning. Their baby sitter is the teenaged daughter of Julie's nursery school teacher. She watches the children and prepares lunch in either the Holland's or the Bishop's home.

Nursery schools are seen by many, though by no means all, parents as an important experience for children. Answers to attitude questions in the NCCCS suggest that parents whose children are in nursery school are more satisfied with their child care arrangements than any other group. When the same survey asked parents if they would prefer a different child care arrangement to the one they were using, more expressed a preference for nursery school than for any other arrangement. Most, however, expressed satisfaction with their current arrangements and did not express any desire to change.[7]

Day Care Centers. The distinction between day care centers and nursery schools has historically followed class lines: poor children went to day care centers while rich children went to nursery school. Analytically, nursery schools are most often distinguished by the presence of an educational program and by the children's attendance for only part of the day; day care centers generally do not offer formal education and are open all day.

When surveys rely on parents to distinguish between day care and nursery school in describing their children's school attendance, one-third of nursery school children were reported to be attending full time —a pattern most people would describe as day care.[8] The NCCCS gave

---

[7] Thomas Ward Rodes and John C. Moore, *National Child Care Consumer Study 1975* (NCCCS), vol. 3, *American Consumer Attitudes and Preferences on Child Care* (Arlington, Va.: Unco, Inc.).

[8] U.S. Bureau of the Census, "Nursery School and Kindergarten Enrollment of

parents both options and found, as shown in Table 2–1, that about 3 percent of those two years old or younger and 5 percent of three-to-five-year-olds are cared for in day care centers, to which should probably be added the 1 percent of those aged two years or less and 3 percent of three-to-five-year-olds reported to be in nursery school more than thirty hours per week.[9] The NCCCS numbers are similar to those found through a survey of licensed day care centers (including full-day nursery schools) and are probably reasonably accurate.

Day care centers are sponsored by a variety of institutions. About 40 percent are profit making; 20 percent are independent nonprofit organizations. The remainder of the nonprofit centers are sponsored by churches (17 percent of all centers), community groups (7 percent), government agencies (7 percent), Head Start (4 percent), schools (3 percent), and other organizations (2 percent).[10]

Most parents whose children are in day care centers are very satisfied with the care their children are receiving. In addition, responses to the NCCCS questions suggest that, as with nursery school, more parents would like to use center care than are now doing so. Among parents of three-to-five-year-olds, almost as many reported that they would prefer day care centers to their present method as were in fact using centers.[11]

Other Nonparental Care. Nine out of ten families with children under fourteen surveyed by the NCCCS in 1975 reported using some form of nonparental, nonschool care for their children. Two-thirds of these

---

Children and Labor Force Status of Their Mothers: October 1967 to October 1976" and "School Enrollment—Social and Economic Characteristics of Students: October 1976," *Current Population Reports*, Series P-20, nos. 318 and 319.

[9] The NCCCS asked respondents whether they agreed or disagreed that "Day care centers and nursery schools are mostly the same thing." Sixty-seven percent of day care users and smaller proportions of users of other care agreed.

[10] These figures are from Craig Coelen, Frederic Glantz, and Daniel Calore, *Day Care Centers in the U.S.: A National Profile, 1976–1977* (Cambridge, Mass.: Abt Associates, 1978).

[11] Rodes and Moore, NCCCS, vol. 3, tables 2–2 and 3–60. One can estimate a maximum preferred distribution for those methods of child care that users most want to switch *to* by assuming that no one wants to switch out. For households with a youngest child aged three to five, users who want to switch would prefer nursery school, day care, and care by a nonrelative in their own home, in that order. The maximum preferred distribution compares with the actual as follows (in percentages):

	Actual	Maximum preferred
Nonrelative in own home	23.9	28.2
Nursery school	11.9	19.8
Day care	7.0	12.3

reported using more than one of the forms of care assessed by the survey.[12]

Table 2–1 suggests that most nonparental care is casual, used for less than ten hours a week. Relatives are used slightly more than non-relatives for casual care; in-home care is somewhat more popular than out-of-home.

Children who are cared for thirty hours a week or more are likely to be outside their own homes in a setting often called family day care. About 7 percent of both those aged two years or less and those aged three to five years are cared for in such an arrangement. The place which full-time family day care can fill in families is illustrated by two cases:

The Johnsons: Mr. and Mrs. Johnson are a young profes-sional couple who combine two full-time careers with caring for their two-year-old son Chad. Mr. Johnson, a senior staff accountant for a national marketing firm, generally works a standard eight-hour day. Mrs. Johnson teaches third grade at a private school, a job which she returned to shortly after her son's birth. Mrs. Johnson's work schedule, like that of her husband, is relatively inflexible from September through May. The Johnson's combined earnings are over $30,000.

Mr. and Mrs. Johnson found a day care home for Chad in a nearby community through a newspaper ad. Chad spends his days in the care of Nancy, a young married woman, and her mother, who together earn their living by tending to five young charges. Mr. Johnson delivers Chad in the morning; Mrs. Johnson picks him up at 4:00 P.M. Since Chad spends so much time during the work week away from his parents, the Johnsons make an effort to include him in their leisure, social, and recreational activities, although they will hire a neighborhood baby sitter for a special evening event.

The Johnsons' values and attitudes regarding maternal em-ployment and child development entered into their day care choices. Mr. Johnson supports his wife's career commitments and actively demonstrates this support by sharing household tasks and child care responsibilities. In addition, both parents feel that Chad benefits by spending his days with other chil-dren—family day care provides independence training while teaching social skills. As a result, they continue to use family care on a reduced basis through the summer when Mrs. Johnson stays at home.

The Sandles: Life is not necessarily simple for the dual-worker couple who depend on full-day child care at only one

---

[12] Rodes and Moore, NCCCS, vol. 1, *Basic Tabulations*.

location. The Sandle family started their son in family day care near their home. Dissatisfied with the situation, they changed to a more desirable setting that cost the same $1.25 an hour but was some distance away. Both facilities belonged to a group of family day care homes sponsored by a local organization of separate community-based day care projects. The central organization recruited caretakers, set up training workshops, and performed check-up visits to caretakers' homes.

Mrs. Sandle is a nurse working a 7:00–3:00 shift. She wakes up at 5:00 A.M. in order to leave for work by 6:00. Her husband and son wake up at 5:30, and Mrs. Sandle gets Benny ready for the day. Father and son leave the house at 7:00 to arrive at Benny's family day care at 7:30. Mr. Sandle then leaves the car at the family day care home, proceeding to work by subway. When her hospital shift is over, Mrs. Sandle takes the subway to the day care home, picks up her son and drives home in the family car. Mr. and Mrs. Sandle both make a point of spending their late afternoons and evenings with Benny. When they do leave him for an occasional evening out, his great aunt frequently acts as an unpaid baby sitter.

Among the perhaps 13 percent of those two years old or younger in full-time nonparental care, about 7 percent are in family day care, 4 percent are cared for in their own homes, and only 2 percent are in nursery schools or day care centers. Among three-to-five-year-olds, the balance reverses; almost as many are in centers and full-time nursery schools (6 percent) as in family day care (7 percent), with only 3 percent cared for full time in their own homes.

For a small proportion of children family day care and baby-sitting, by both relatives and nonrelatives, substitute during the day for parents. In addition, it is clear from the very high rates of casual usage that extended family, neighborhood, and market arrangements are extremely important supplements to the care provided by parents and schools.

Patterns. The data available on child care arrangements in the United States suggest the importance of families and schools as caretakers. They also suggest that the overwhelming majority of families supplement parental and school care with at least one, and usually more than one, regular nonparental care arrangement. Surprisingly small proportions of children spend thirty hours a week or more in nonparental, nonschool care arrangements.

Nonparental care for children under three is most likely to be

29

home care, provided partly by relatives and partly by nonrelatives. Among three-to-five-year-olds, the balance shifts to formal care, with nursery school and kindergarten, day care centers and family day care becoming more popular. For six-to-thirteen-year-olds, public school is the major caretaker, supplemented by parents and other arrangements.[13] These patterns vary surprisingly little by race or economic status of parents.[14] They suggest that age of child and idiosyncratic decisions of families are the most important determining factors. How these determinations are made by parents—the calculation of costs and benefits— is taken up in the next section.

Sharing the Burdens of Child Care

It is clear that child care is a costly enterprise, not only in money. The case studies of families in the previous section illustrate the time, energy, and concern—as well as money and forgone consumer goods—that many families invest in their children. Less well illustrated in these cases are the costs borne by society as a whole. This section examines these costs, first to families and then to government, of caring for children.

Private Costs. Some families pay for their child care in the forgone earnings and missed career opportunities of a parent, usually of the mother who stays home to care for children. Some pay in complicated work schedules or night work. Some pay in money, energy, time, and consistency of parenting styles. For all families, the costs of child care are high. Most often forgotten in discussions of child care are the costs to families in which one parent remains at home to care for children. Only about 30 percent of mothers with children under fourteen were working full time in the paid labor force in 1976.[15] For the other 70 percent of families, the forgone earnings of the mother constitute the major cost of child care. Since women have different potential earnings, these costs vary from family to family but are clearly substantial.

The NCCCS provides some data on the more straightforward costs of child care. Respondents who used nonparental child care at least one

---

[13] I am grateful to Sheila Kammerman and Alfred Kahn for persistently and persuasively calling my attention to the importance of age differences. For an excellent discussion, see Sheila B. Kammerman and Alfred J. Kahn, "The Day Care Debate: A Wider View," Cross National Studies of Social Services and Family Policy (Columbia University School of Social Work, 1978; processed).

[14] Race and income differences are reported in Rodes and Moore, NCCCS, vol. 2, *Current Patterns of Child Care Use in the United States.*

[15] Hayghe, "Marital and Family Characteristics of Workers."

hour a week were asked if they paid for it, either in cash or in exchanged services or favors. Of the respondents 10.6 percent reported no payment, 55.2 percent paid in cash, and 54.5 percent exchanged services or favors (some clearly both paid cash and exchanged favors). Differences in cost according to the main method of child care used are shown in Table 2–6. The total cost of nonparental child care paid by parents was estimated by the NCCCS at $6.3 billion.

In making decisions many families clearly weigh cash costs against the nonmonetary costs of exchanges. For example, one recently employed mother in the Families and Communities Project reports that she used to be involved in "all kinds of trading when the kids were smaller. Now I don't want to pay back the obligation. I want to spend any free time that I have with my children and not baby-sitting for someone else's child." As a result this working mother would now prefer to "hire and pay rather than ask friends and neighbors." The Working Family Project and the Families and Communities Project data suggest that informal baby-sitting exchanges among parents work best when mothers do not work or work short hours. When mothers put in long work hours, they find it increasingly difficult and onerous to contribute their share to cooperative arrangements. Rather than being in debt to their neighbors and friends, they seem to prefer paying in cash at least for their regular child care arrangements.

Other costs are even more subtle. Some families pay by giving up their privacy when they enroll their children in formal, particularly government-subsidized programs. For example, one family from the Working Family Project complained that their involvement at one day care center required detailed discussions with other parents of child care strategies. This, they felt, should remain a private family matter. (Other parents, of course, would value such opportunities for discussion.)

Child care arrangements can come at the expense of other aspects of family life. With the use of outside care, children may spend relatively little time in the company of their parents, and that limited time usually occurs at the end of long, active days when both children and parents are tired and irritable. Some parents counter this situation by spending most of their leisure time (weekends, holidays, early evenings) with their children, rather than socializing with other adults, thus increasing their feeling of isolation. Another cost for parents is the lack of consistent care and discipline received by their children across settings. This is not just an issue of inside-the-home care versus outside-the-home care. Parents who work staggered hours are usually with their children at different times, and the husband and wife may develop divergent styles of parenting. Parents who use outside-the-home care or

31

TABLE 2–6
Costs of Child Care, by Mode and Type of Payment, for All Users of Child Care

Mode	Percent Paying			Total Estimated Annual National Consumer Cost (millions of dollars)	Average Cash Cost for Those Who Pay Cash	
	Nothing	In cash	In services		Dollars per service hour	Dollars per week
Relative, own home	22.7	16.1	61.2	464.7	0.35	10.52
Nonrelative, own home	6.7	80.4	12.9	1,679.4	0.53	7.78
Relative, other home	22.4	12.4	65.2	674.1	0.39	14.24
Nonrelative, other home	8.2	43.7	48.1	1,790.4	0.54	16.07
Nursery school	15.8	80.3	3.9	1,044.6	0.66	14.59
Day care center	12.7	77.5	9.7	547.1	0.57	19.56
Parent cooperative	14.7	17.1	68.2	17.1	N.A.	N.A.
Before- and after-school care	57.7	28.3	14.0	101.5	N.A.	N.A.
Head Start	79.8	2.8	17.3	—	—	—
All modes	10.6	55.2	54.5	6,321.6	—	14.73

Dash (—): Not applicable.
N.A.: Not available.
SOURCE: Rodes and Moore, NCCCS, vol. 1, table IV–1, and vol. 2, tables VIII–1, VIII–3, and VIII–4.

even in-home baby sitters or relatives may feel that consistency remains an issue for them and their child and is a price they most often pay for child care arrangements.

Weighing Costs and Benefits. The enormous variations in what parents pay for child care in money, time, energy, consistency, and forgone opportunities suggest that the cost-benefit trade-off is extremely complicated. There is no low-cost child care: the question for parents is how much they will pay in each currency.

Notions of child development clearly enter parents' calculations, and many parents make substantial sacrifices to provide the kind of care they consider the most appropriate. Families differ substantially in what they think is best for children, especially between the ages of three and five. These differences do not follow neat class lines but instead reflect the different values held by individuals in the society. One family interviewed by the Working Family Project expressed considerable dismay at the educational content of many child care programs: children are too young to be pressured into that type of activity; time enough when they are school age. Other parents, like the Stephens and the Gardners, highly value the preschool programs available and feel they lead to enriched cognitive and social development. Nationally, 22.7 percent agreed and 28.4 percent were neutral in response to an NCCCS statement: "There is too much stress placed on trying to teach children things in most places where children are taken care of."[16]

Parents also differ in the extent to which they want their young children to be involved with a group of peers. For some families, it seems important to give preschoolers experience with their peers, particularly in the case of an only child or the only preschool-aged child in the family. For this reason, many parents, like the Bishops, arrange play groups or enroll their children in some organized program. For other parents, however, the peer group is a societal force to be feared as an unknown and put off for as long as possible. Parents feel that as children enter a peer group, parental influence diminishes, and children are exposed to behavior and values that are certainly different from and perhaps unacceptable to the family. Perceptions of parental career lines also affect decisions. In most of the families interviewed in the Working Family Project and Families and Communities Project, wives are carrying primary responsibility for the care of young children. This is not to say that husbands are not major contributors in many of these families, but when the chips are down, the women are responsible for

---

[16] Rodes and Moore, NCCCS, vol. 3, table 3–48.

seeing that children are being properly supervised. They tend to locate the care; they tend to work off hours or interrupt careers if that seems necessary; they stay home with a sick child and answer emergency calls from day care providers.

Because women in these families stand behind the child care their children receive, all decisions about child care are usually construed in terms of pay-offs against the value of the mother's employment, both in terms of the financial costs and benefits and in terms of the value the mother puts on her work activities.

To those working toward a career, it may seem more reasonable to make a heavy investment in child care to allow the work to continue through the early childhood years. This investment may be made in terms of money, in terms of energy and emotional strain, or some combination of the two. For example, Mrs. Bishop from the Families and Communities Project is willing to hire child care, considering it an investment necessary to building her own business.

For women who are working in a static status situation, there is less impetus to enter into complex employment and child care arrangements simply to hold onto that particular job. It makes much more sense to seek a different job with different hours or more flexibility than to pay a great deal for child care. Many women like Mrs. Wyatt and Mrs. Stephens enter the labor force because their family is in need of their earnings. That is their primary motivating factor. For these women, it makes little sense to pay over a large amount of their earnings for child care when those earnings are the reason for working in the first place.

In sum, the well-being of the family, both parents and children, seems to be the main goal of parents in making decisions about child care. The costs are high, but the benefits are high as well. Families pay the costs in different currencies and weigh them against different kinds of benefits. These complicated calculations to some extent explain the diversity of institutions described in the first section.

Public Costs. Not all of the costs of child care are borne by families. The most substantial public costs arise from completely subsidized public schooling. The public also bears a share of the cost of caring for children below school age by subsidizing parental and other kinds of care through government spending programs and the tax system. Various levels of government are also heavily involved in regulating, and for older children providing, child care.

Parents. The major public subsidy for child care that goes to parents is the tax exemption for dependents, a tax expenditure worth about $200 per child in 1977. The money saved in taxes can, of course, be spent however families wish. Another provision of the tax code, which allows income splitting by married couples, more directly encourages parental care. The provision provides a tax advantage to one earner (or two grossly disparate earners) vis-à-vis two-earner families, thus partly mitigating the financial cost of forgone earnings. Not all families who take advantage of the income-splitting provisions have children, of course. These provisions are a very indirect and loose subsidy for parental care, but they are so large a tax expenditure that they deserve consideration.

Schools. In 1977 federal, state, and local governments spent about $72.9 billion on public elementary and secondary education.[17] Private schools receive almost no public subsidy, with the exception of certain services—transportation, textbooks, and so on. School budgets usually include kindergartens and in some districts prekindergarten as well. The federal government subsidizes Head Start for prekindergarten children, some preschool programs for disadvantaged children under Title I, and some preschool education for handicapped children (see Table 2–7).

Other child care institutions. The costs of nonparental, nonschool child care are also shared by the public, though to a much lesser extent than the costs of schooling. How public and private sharing of cost and responsibility works can be seen by examining child care services within one community. Table 2-7 presents information on the child care services to children under six years of age in Claremont, a medium-sized town of mixed ethnic and class composition in Massachusetts (total 1970 population, 54,000), on which the Families and Communities Project has gathered information. Claremont was chosen for the study in large part because it has an established and well-developed system of family services, including child care. The bulk of formal services are for children over three years of age; there are no group programs for younger children.

The table indicates the many different services in Claremont supported by government funding. However, the restrictions on the various categories of public funds means that most families are limited in their choice of arrangements. For example, Head Start can be used only by poor families, families just over the income guidelines with special health, social, or learning problems, or families of handicapped children. (By law, 10 percent of the clients must be handicapped.) While a sizable number of families express interest in the program (all welfare

[17] U.S. Bureau of the Census, *Statistical Abstract of the United States 1977* (Washington, D.C., 1977), table 202.

35

TABLE 2–7
Child Care Services in Claremont, Massachusetts, Children Six Years or Older

Name	Program	Sponsorship	Profit/ Nonprofit	Number of Children	Funding Source	Dollar Amount
Richards Day Center	Four family day care homes; one group day care; full day	Independent	Nonprofit	54—11 family day care; 43 group care	Title XX (33 slots)	88,623
					Claremont School Department (2 slots)	7,185
					School lunch program	13,200
					State Office for Children	695
					State Department of Special Education	5,600
					Parent fees	42,150
					Local charities and contributions	9,194
					Two CETA[a] employees	
					Total	166,647
Claremont Children's Center	One group day care; full and part day	Independent	Nonprofit	52 total (30 full-time equivalents)	One CETA[a] employee	70,000
					Parent fees	
					Local charities and contributions	900
					Total	70,900
Family day care homes[b]	Full and part day; sixteen homes	Independent	Profit	64	Parent fees	166,400[c]
Baby-sitting services	Parent-arranged child care[d]	Independent	Profit	Title XX: 20[e] Private: No available information	Title XX	52,000 (est.)
					Private	No available information

Program	Type of program	Sponsor	Status	Enrollment	Funding source	Budget
Head Start	Part day (9:00-1:00), school year; medical, social, and developmental	Head Start	Nonprofit	30 part time	Head Start One CETA employee	54,000
Happy Times Nursery School	Cooperative; part day (9:00-11:30), school year	Church	Nonprofit	46 part time	Parent fees	14,868
Claremont Heights Nursery	Part day (9:00-11:30), nursery school year	Church	Nonprofit	48 part time	Parent fees Local fund-raising	Not available 15,000 (est.)
Pinecrest School	Two- or three-hour nursery; high school development training classes	Claremont School Department	Nonprofit	36 part time	Parent Fees State Division of Occupational Education grant Claremont Public School Department	4,680 20,000 Space and salaries for two teachers; dollar amounts not available
Claremont public schools	Kindergarten half day[f]	Claremont School Department	Nonprofit	350	One CETA employee Claremont Public School Department	No estimate

[a] Comprehensive Employment and Training Act.

[b] In Massachusetts, those who care for one or more children other than their own in their own home are required to register with the Office of Children and meet minimum space, health, and safety requirements. There is no reliable estimate of the number of family day care homes that, despite the law, are not registered.

[c] Estimate based on full use, at $1.25 an hour for forty hours a week.

[d] There are no available data on nonfunded baby-sitting arrangements or on baby-sitting costs that are computed as part of a recipient's Aid to Families with Dependent Children allotment.

[e] Regulations allow payments to relatives if they live outside the immediate household; however, the local office is apparently lax about enforcing such a restriction.

[f] For children five years old as of January 1 of the year preceding school enrollment.

SOURCE: Families and Communities Project.

recipients are eligible), the local Head Start can serve only about a third of those parents who apply.

Parents are also restricted in their choice of a full day care program. Families with incomes slightly above the Title XX requirements (recipients of Aid to Families with Dependent Children, AFDC, or equivalent) might not be able to afford full-time day care at Richards Day School or the Claremont Children's Center, where prices range upward of $50 per week.[18]

There are only thirty-three Title XX–funded day care slots, although Claremont has more than 700 families who earn less than 125 percent of the poverty level and have children under six. (Title XX of the Social Security Act provides grants to states for social services to past, current, and potential welfare recipients.) These factors limit a family's choices in several ways. First, if an eligible family wants their child to participate in a group day care program, they must go to the one center with a Title XX contract. They cannot choose among the noncontracted facilities that offer child care. Even if they decide they would like to enroll their child in the contracted program, however, they may not be free to do so. The Welfare Department reports that more than twenty Title XX eligible families are on the Richards Day Center waiting list, or more than half again as many as the thirty-three slots available. Some of these waiting families receive temporary Title XX baby-sitting funds, which they can use to pay a private caretaker of their own choosing. These funds, however, are also limited, since they cannot be used to pay a relative who is living in the family's own household. Other families might delay a parent's employment until they can be sure of their child's placement in an appropriate facility. Still others might opt to list child care costs as an allowable expense in their AFDC budget arrangements, and thus pay for private baby-sitting services or perhaps unlicensed family care, although technically it is illegal in the state of Massachusetts.

Since federal funds are primarily available only in Head Start and the Richards Day Center, there are great differences in the class composition of Claremont's child care services. Richards, despite its waiting list for Title XX families, has trouble finding private-paying parents who can use its services and, like Head Start, serves primarily low-income families. The Claremont Children's Center, in contrast, has mostly upper-middle-income families, as do the privately operated local nursery schools.

Several important questions about child care services in Claremont

---

[18] Day care in the state of Massachusetts is more expensive than the national average. There is fairly strict adherence to state and federal day care regulations.

have not been addressed. First, the table does not distinguish between regular preschoolers and those with special needs. Several of the formal programs include children who receive outside support services for their special needs. Next, it is difficult to estimate the number of parents who rely on informal services, such as child care provided by relatives, and whether they pay for such services in cash or in kind. It is also difficult to estimate the number of unlicensed family day care homes. We are unable to determine how much additional federal money is spent on child care through the AFDC program. The local welfare office does not keep records on the amount of child care deducted as an allowable expense in the determination of individual families' AFDC payments. Nor are we able to estimate the contribution made by CETA (Comprehensive Employment and Training Act) in the form of child care staff. Finally, we do not know how many families make use of the child care tax credit.

Despite this missing information, however, the impact of government involvement on child care services in Claremont is clear. The child care provided by the Claremont school department, especially kindergarten, is extremely important, as is the availability of federal and other funding for child care programs.

Child Care and Government Nationally

Funding. Table 2–8 shows the more important federal programs that provide funds for child care or preschool education. The largest in terms of budget allocations are Head Start, child care services provided for current and potential AFDC recipients under Title XX (grants to states for social services) of the Social Security Act, and the tax expenditure generated by the credit for dependent care.[19]

Coelen and others report that 25 percent of the children enrolled

---

[19] We are perfectly comfortable with the notion of tax expenditures when they result, as this one does, from an explicit change in the tax code for the purpose of benefiting certain groups. There are, however, two serious problems with this particular tax expenditure. First, the estimated cost may not be anywhere near accurate since the figures in the budget were estimated without any apparent reference to actual tax returns. Second, it can be argued that child care is a legitimate business expense that should never have been taxed in the first place by a system that purports to tax net rather than gross income. This argument would also seem to require, however, that the portion of federal spending for day care (such as Title XX and Head Start) that represents business expenses for workers ought to be considered part of recipients' gross, but not net, income, equivalent to a refundable tax credit of 100 percent rather than a social service expenditure. We are not sure how to deal with this argument and thus have settled for the definitions of budget and tax expenditure items used by the Office of Management and Budget.

in day care centers are paid for by government funds (not including tax credits).[20] Of the total revenues of day care centers, 29 percent come from government,[21] which suggests that about a third of government child care funds go to day care centers. The proportion of total spending on child care that comes from government is more difficult to determine. An estimate can be derived by using NCCCS's estimated national consumer costs of child care, $6.32 billion annually.[22] Dividing total nonschool federal spending (about $1.58 billion, excluding tax credits) · by estimated consumer spending plus total federal spending (assuming that consumers do not report government spending on their behalf as spending) suggests that almost 20 percent of all nonschool child care cash costs are paid by the federal government.

Government funds are paid out in various ways. Head Start money goes in the form of grants to public and private nonprofit agencies, which in turn provide comprehensive preschool programs in accordance with federal Head Start guidelines. Title XX money goes to states (usually the Department of Public Welfare) which spend in accordance with their own state plans. The tax credit can be claimed by individuals for any form of paid, work-related child care, even that provided by a relative in the child's home as long as that relative is not also claimed as a dependent. Thus, federal funding does not imply federal or other government provision of services, and only in certain cases does it imply federal regulation. As now structured, federal funding supports a diverse set of child care arrangements.

Licensing and Regulation. All fifty states require licensing of day care centers, variously defined by some minimum number of children. Most states also purport to require licensing of family day care homes (defined in even more varying ways), but it is not clear that these requirements are enforced. State licensing requirements generally cover physical space, health, and safety. All states except Mississippi also set minimum ratios of adult staff to children that centers must adhere to. The re-

---

[20] Coelen and others, *Day Care Centers in the U.S.*, table 20, p. 57.

[21] Rodes and Moore, NCCCS, vol. 1, table 3–31.

[22] Rodes and Moore, NCCCS, vol. 2, table 8–1. The NCCCS estimate of the total amount that parents pay to day care centers nationally ($547.1 million) is only about 60 percent of what Coelen and others estimate that day care centers receive from parent fees ($900.4 million). The discrepancy is not likely to be accounted for by the fact that Coelen collected data a year later than Rodes and Moore. We are inclined to consider Coelen's estimates more accurate. This suggests that NCCCS estimates of total spending on child care, of which spending on day care accounts for 8.7 percent, are probably underestimated by some unknown amount. Thus our estimate of the government share is probably an overestimate, also by some unknown amount.

TABLE 2–8

FEDERAL FUNDS FOR CHILD CARE, FISCAL YEAR 1977

Program (Agency)	Number of Children Served (thousands)	Estimated Obligations for Child Care or Preschool (millions of dollars)
Title XX social services grants to states— portion used for child care for low- and moderate-income families (HEW)	799	809
Head Start—comprehensive preschool for low-income children (HEW)	349	448
ESEA[a] Title I—compensatory preschool and kindergarten for disadvantaged children (HEW)	367	136
Child Care Food Service Program (Agriculture)	580	120
AFDC[b]—welfare benefit increases to subsidize work-related child care costs (HEW)	145	84
AFDC/WIN[c]—child care services for welfare recipients participating in WIN (HEW)	85	57
Other direct programs	466	99
Child care tax credit—20 percent of work-related expenses; limit of $400 for one child and $800 for two or more children (Treasury)	4,000	500
Total		2,252

NOTE: Components do not add to total because of rounding.

[a] Elementary and Secondary Education Act.

[b] Aid to Families with Dependent Children.

[c] Work Incentive program.

SOURCE: Congressional Budget Office, *Childcare and Preschool: Options for Federal Support* (Washington, D.C., 1978).

quired child-staff ratios, which generally differ for different ages, vary tremendously from state to state. For example, Rhode Island requires one adult for every five three-year-olds, while Ohio allows an adult-child ratio of one to fifteen for three-year-olds.[23]

---

[23] Data on licensing requirements and on center compliance from Coelen and others, *Day Care Centers in the U.S.*, pp. 69–96.

In addition to state licensing requirements, centers that receive federal funding are expected to comply with federal regulations (Federal Interagency Day Care Requirements, or FIDCR). The FIDCR cover staff-child ratios, maximum group size, nutrition (provision of meals), required health exams, social services, counseling on child development, and parent participation. Minimum staff-child ratios under FIDCR are 1:4 for children aged two and under, 1:5 for three-year-olds, 1:7 for four- to five-year-olds, and 1:15 for six- to nine-year-olds. (Most schools would not meet these FIDCR ratios, a fact that has not escaped the attention of Congress.)

Coelen and others report that 44 percent of day care centers, enrolling 45 percent of all day care children, receive some federal funding and should therefore comply with the FIDCR. Their data on staff-child ratios suggest that 68 percent of the centers receiving federal funds and 37 percent of those not receiving federal funds actually comply with the FIDCR staffing standards.[24] The study also suggests that a majority of centers, whether covered by FIDCR or not, also comply with federal regulations on group size, meals, required health exams, counseling, and community service. A majority of the centers receiving federal funds also comply with FIDCR parent participation standards, but other centers are less likely to.[25] Virtually all the centers surveyed comply with the staffing requirements of their own states, which, of course, are usually more lenient than the federal.

The NCCCS reports that 97.1 percent of the children in day care centers are in licensed facilities, as are 86.0 percent of the children in nursery or preschool. However, only 10.3 percent of the children cared for by a nonrelative in the other person's home were in licensed facilities, while 31.2 percent of all children in the three types of nonrelative out-of-home care were in licensed care.[26]

Provision. Very little nonschool child care is actually provided by government. Coelen and others estimated that 3.2 percent of day care centers are sponsored by a school and 7.0 percent by a government agency. Nursery school is more often provided by government: as noted earlier, 31 percent of nursery school students are in public facilities. Schooling for older children is dominated by government; 85

---

[24] Ibid., figure 1, p. 26, table 4, p. 32. In 1976 Congress placed a moratorium on the enforcement of FIDCR staff-child ratio requirements in day care centers receiving Title XX funds. Title XX centers were, however, forbidden to raise their ratios above 1975 levels. Moreover, centers receiving other federal funds were not excused from the enforcement of the FIDCR.

[25] Ibid., table 29, p. 80.

[26] Rodes and Moore, NCCCS, vol. 1.

percent of kindergarten children and 90 percent of elementary school children are in public schools.

Issues for the Future

The current variety of child care institutions and the sharing of costs and responsibilities between the public and private sector have developed over a period of years. The future course of that development— the allocation of the responsibility for and costs of child care among different public and private institutions—is the current policy issue.

The policy options available to the federal government can be examined for the four different forms of governmental involvement in child care:

- Public provision: public schools, kindergartens, and preschool programs and some Head Start programs
- Public funding and regulation: most Head Start programs and Title XX day care
- Public funding without regulation: tax credit for dependent care and AFDC work expense allowance
- General public subsidy of children: tax exemption for dependents and income-splitting provisions.

Table 2–9 shows the policy options that the Congressional Budget Office (CBO) considers possible directions for the future. Because these build on current policy, each emphasizes one of the above forms of governmental involvement. In addition to these options, Congress could also cut back on programs, thus shifting a larger proportion of the costs of child care to parents. Alternatively, Congress could consider a general subsidy to children, in the form of a child-allowance, child tax credit, or mothers' wages.

The extent of public assumption of the costs of child care is clearly the most important underlying issue in the debate about child care policy. On the one hand, Americans have historically paid for the education of children aged five to sixteen with public funds. On the other hand, a long tradition of parental rights and responsibilities, especially regarding young children, argues against increased governmental participation.

Despite the famous Nixon veto of the Comprehensive Child Development Bill, the years since 1971 have seen dramatic growth in government funding and provision of child care. Kindergarten attendance has grown dramatically, implying that more local communities are providing such services. Head Start has grown. Federally funded day care for the poor has grown. The child care tax credit has been written into the law. All these programs are more likely to grow than to go away. On the other hand, given the current emphasis on budget austerity, a major legislative initiative for day care is not likely in the next few years, nor is the general balance between public and private costs likely to change very much. There may, however, be program changes which affect the balance among public, parental, and private nonparental provisions of care. The issues are likely to arise in two areas, preschool education and tax-transfer policy.

Preschool Education. Discussion of preschool education may well be precipitated by the Education for All Handicapped Children Act (PL 94-142), which is likely to provide a new and dramatic impetus to the growth of the nursery schools and kindergartens. This law, effective September 1978, requires states to provide free, appropriate education for all handicapped children beginning at age three. The law provides federal matching funds to help states meet the requirements; these funds in themselves will substantially increase spending on preschool programs. It will be interesting to see whether the money has a multiplier effect as well: whether communities decide to expand preschool for the nonhandicapped at the same time they are establishing their mandated programs for the handicapped.

It will also be interesting to see how PL 94-142 preschool programs are set up. They might be like kindergartens, run almost entirely by and in public schools. They might be like Head Start, sponsored by a wide range of government, community, and private groups. They might be like Title XX day care in some states, with the states buying slots for handicapped children in a wide variety of settings which serve fee-paying clients as well. They might even follow the analogy of the tax credit, by providing vouchers for parents to spend as they wish.

What happens with PL 94-142 is important not just for handicapped children but for the child care system as a whole, since it may tilt the balance in preschool education toward—or away from—public provision. The location of the Bureau for the Education of the Handicapped in the Office of Education may be presumed to favor public school sponsorship. The opportunity exists, however, to encourage the continued development of facilities run by private groups, churches, neighborhood organizations, and parents themselves. This could set an important precedent for preschool education generally.

As the country moves toward more widespread provision of nursery school, a related issue, which may be first defined in terms of the handicapped, is whether preschool is perceived as voluntary or com-

TABLE 2–9

Costs and Impacts of Alternatives to Current Federal Child Care Policies

Option	Incremental Federal Cost (billions of dollars)	Change in Number of Children Served (millions)	Recipient Population	Targeted Mode of Care	Possible Developmental Effects
Expand Head Start to all eligibles	2.0	1.2	Low income	Comprehensive preschool	Positive if well planned
Expand Title XX	1.0	0.2	Low and moderate income	Licensed care	Modest
Expand tax credit	0.7	Uncertain	All except higher income	At discretion of recipient	Low
Categorical day care/ preschool initiative (3- and 4-year-olds)	4–9	2–4	All income groups[a]	Licensed care or preschool	Greatest effect among low-income children
Before- and after-school care (6- to 13-year-olds)	3–6.5	7–19	All income groups[a]	Schools	None intended
Induced effects of welfare reform	0	0–0.2	Low and moderate income	At discretion of recipient	Low

[a] These programs could be targeted to low- and middle-income families by adjusting fees according to the ability of parents to pay for services. Instituting such a fee schedule would reduce costs.

Source: Same as Table 2–8.

pulsory. The data presented in the first section of this paper suggest that genuine differences of opinion exist in the population about the appropriate age when children should enter nonfamily care or educational settings. Given these differences, it is striking that nearly all eligible children attend kindergarten, even though it is nowhere compulsory. Can it be that all parents consider their children ready for school at age four and a half or five? Or since kindergarten is provided by the public schools is it perceived as part of that system and therefore necessary for children? Do schools pressure parents to send children to kindergarten by hinting that it really is compulsory or by designing school assignment systems that reward kindergarten attendance?

A state requirement that three- and four-year-olds attend school would certainly be opposed by most Americans as unwarranted intervention in parental rights. But a de facto requirement, perceived as such by parents, might become quietly established if the public schools capture the growing nursery school market. To preserve parent choice and to strengthen nongovernmental community organizations it will be important to encourage diversity in sponsorship and to assure parents that attendance at nursery school is in fact a choice.

Welfare Reform. Every attempt to reform the welfare system—and one is bound to succeed sooner or later—must confront questions about child care. The questions are especially pressing in light of the recent proposals to require work and guarantee jobs for welfare recipients. The Carter administration's version of welfare reform would exclude from the work requirement single parents responsible for preschool children, thus avoiding both the costs of day care and the necessity of providing jobs for these parents. Single parents of school-age children would be required to accept part-time jobs, or full-time jobs if adequate after-school care were available. The Carter plan can be thought of as a method for paying parents to care for their own young children.

No welfare reform in the near future is likely to include a requirement that mothers of preschool children work: the costs of providing day care and creating jobs are simply too high. The issue of what to do about mothers who want to work, however, is not satisfactorily settled. Should those mothers who want to work be provided jobs and day care? Should they be provided jobs but left to find day care on their own, deducting the costs from their earnings for the purpose of calculating their grants? What constraints, if any, should be placed on these day care choices—the strict regulations of Title XX day care or the loose coverage of the tax credit?

Tax Credits. Perhaps the most likely direction for child care policy in the next few years is toward increases in tax credits. One possibility is for the tax credit for dependent care to be raised to cover a higher percentage of child care costs and to be made refundable. (The estimated cost of expanding the tax credit in the CBO report is based on a refundable credit of 50 percent of work-related child care costs, with a family income ceiling.) Another possibility is for the current exemption for dependents to become a tax credit. If the credit were refundable, this would be equivalent to a child-allowance.

Using tax credits for child care policy is appealing in several ways. Tax expenditure programs seem more likely to be passed by Congress than spending programs, since their costs are largely hidden. Tax credits provide benefits to large proportions of the population, another politically attractive feature. From the point of view of child care institutions, tax credits provide maximum flexibility and maximum parental choice. Families can use their tax credits to subsidize any kind of care, or combination of methods, that they think most appropriate for their children.

Public Choices. It is clear that child care policy must face a number of issues besides that of the level of publicly financed subsidy vis-à-vis private costs. Whatever the level of support, program choices can affect the balance among parental provision of child care, school, and child care provided by extended family, community organizations, and the market.

Tilting the balance more toward the school would seem to be undesirable on several counts. Public schools already monopolize a large proportion of children's time. Their institutional structure and history has made them relatively unresponsive to parental preferences. Allowing the schools to become important providers of care for three- to five-year-old children could result in their replacing the rich variety of institutions that now exist to supplement parents and schools in providing child care.

In contrast, there are obvious advantages to enhancing the role of parents in making child care choices, whether through tax credits for work-related child care or through universal refundable child tax credits. Both these devices transfer some of the costs of child care to the society as a whole (and children are, after all, a societal resource) while leaving the responsibility for choosing child care with parents. They thus enhance the power of families both by increasing their available resources and thus their bargaining power in the market, and by permitting parents to choose child care that reflects their own values and preferences.

47

There may also be a role, however, for some government funding directed specifically toward encouraging the growth of nonparental, non-school child care institutions. Nursery schools, Head Start centers, day care centers, and family day care homes play important roles in the care of three- to five-year-old children and are very popular with parents. They operate under a variety of church, community, and private auspices, and their dramatic recent growth has surely been encouraged by the federally regulated and funded programs described above.

Tax credits or child-allowances might well be used by parents to maintain these institutions, and if those allowances were generous enough, additional subsidies might not be necessary. If markets prove unresponsive, however, and if allowances remain low, continued government support may be needed to preserve the institutional diversity that now characterizes child care in the United States.

In short, examination of existing patterns suggests an intricate balance between public and private, and among family, school, and other institutions. Future policy will have some effect on this balance, especially if it were to shift strongly toward schools or toward families. Maintenance of the balance may require continuation of some parts of the messy, complex set of programs that now exist. Neither the program nor the institutional structures are neat, but in that may lie the vitality of the system.

Appendix

The term "child care" is used in this paper in an inclusive sense, covering all the arrangements made for the care of children under age fourteen, in home and out of home, parental and nonparental, formal and informal, public and private. To describe child care in this broad sense, we use data from four surveys and two ethnographic sources:

1. The Bureau of the Census, as part of its regular Current Population Survey, collects data each October on the school enrollment of the population aged three and over. At the same time, data are collected on family income, the labor force status of household members, and other demographic characteristics. The sample includes about 50,000 households. The data used in this paper are reported in two publications in the Current Population Reports series: U.S. Bureau of the Census, "Nursery School and Kindergarten Enrollment of Children and Labor Force Status of Their Mothers: October 1967 to October 1976," *Current Population Reports*, Series P-20, no. 318; and "School Enrollment—Social and Economic Characteristics of Students: October 1976," *Current Population Reports*, Series P-20, no. 319.

2. As a supplement to the regular Current Population Survey in October 1974, the Census Bureau asked a question about the day care of children aged seven to thirteen. In February 1975, three questions were added to the Current Population Survey on the daytime care of children aged three to six. The data are reported in U.S. Bureau of the Census, "Daytime Care of Children: October 1974 and February 1975," *Current Population Reports*, Series P-20, no. 298. The 1974 survey question was "What kind of arrangements (other than school) were made for the day time care of [child] during the last two weeks: Cared for in day care center at parent's expense; None; Child cares for self; Cared for in own home by other relatives; Cared for in own home by non-relative; Cared for in relative's home; Cared for in non-relative's home at the expense of parent; Cared for in non-relative's home not at the expense of parent; Other?" The 1975 survey questions were: "Who cares for [child] during the day (when [child] is not in school): Mother; Father; Child cares for self; Other relative; Nonrelative? Does the family pay for this care? Where is [child] care for: Parent's home; Someone else's home; Day care center?"

3. In the *National Child Care Consumer Study* (NCCCS), Thomas Ward Rodes and John C. Moore gathered information on the child care arrangements of over 4,500 households with children under fourteen years during the spring and early summer of 1975. In-depth personal interviews were designed to elicit information on patterns of child care arrangements, not only the methods and hours of use but also parental attitudes and preferences. The study was prepared for the Department of Health, Education, and Welfare, Office of Child Development.

4. The National Day Care Supply Study (Coelen and others, *Day Care Centers in the U.S.*) collected data on 3,167 day care centers, about 16 percent of all licensed centers in the United States. Data were collected by telephone in 1976 and 1977 on the characteristics of the center and of the children enrolled.

5. The Working Family Project, funded by the National Institute of Mental Health and the National Institute of Education, collected data over a two-year period (1973–1975) from twenty-five middle-income families in the greater Boston area. Work with each family included a series of intensive interviews with parents, and in some cases with grandparents and children; a series of observations in the home; and a number of paper and pencil tasks. The team of sociologists, anthropologists, and psychologists working with dual-worker families included principal investigator Laura Lein; administrator Janet Lennon; research

49

TABLE 2-10
DEMOGRAPHIC CHARACTERISTICS OF WFP AND FCP FAMILIES

Family	Sex (age) of Children	Approximate Family Income	Mother's Work Hours	Father's Work Hours	Relatives in Boston	Care Used In-Home[a]	Care Used Out-of-Home
1974–1975 figures for WFP							
Wyatt	M (6) M (4)	$18,000	8–5	Rotating shift, often 7–4	Yes		Nursery school School Neighbor
Hunt	M (6) M (3)	$20,000	3–11	8:30–5	Yes	Baby sitter Husband alone	Kindergarten Day care center
Sandle	M (3)	$10,000	7–3:30	8:30–5	Yes		Family day care
Den	F (4)	$13,000	8:30–5 approx.	7–3:30	Yes	With mother (running day care home)	Nursery school
Henry	F (4) F (2)	$12,000	4–10	8–4	Yes		Neighbor
1977 figures for FCP							
Johnson[b]	M (2)	More than $30,000	8:30–4	9–5	No		Family day care
Gardner	M (5)	More than $20,000	Currently not working	Variable, long days	No		Nursery school
Bishop[b]	M (7) F (3)	More than $20,000	9–2 approx.	8–4, several evenings	No		School Nursery school

50

Stephens	F (3)	More than $35,000	Currently not working	8:30–6	Yes	Nursery school
Irving	M (18) F (15) M (13)	More than $20,000	8:30–2:30	9–5	Yes	School

[a] Care by primary caretaker, the mother, is not listed.
[b] Schedules presented are for the academic year.

TABLE 2–11
CHILD CARE ARRANGEMENTS OF WFP FAMILIES

	Out-of-Home							In-Home			
Family	Nursery school	Day care center	Kinder-garten	School	Day care home/ neighbor	Play-group	Baby sitter	Relative, non-nuclear	Husband alone	Older chil-dren	Mother works at home
Chapin		A 9:30–5:30			B 3 ams + 2 pms	B 2 ams					
Beer		A 8:30–5:30									
Charles		A 9–5									
Deneux									Odd times		A+B some eves
Farlane				A–C 8–2					A–C eves +alt. Sun.		
Ben		A 2:30–5 or 6		A 8–2:30							
Foster				A–C 8–3							
Henry							A+B 3x/wk 3 eves/wk		A+B 2 eves		
Hunt							A+B 3–5 pms		A+B eves		
Heyman	A 8–12	B 1 am/wk	A ams								A pms
Jackson				A–E 8–3					A–E some on wkends		

Family							
James							A ams + pms
Long		A 10–3				A+B 10–2 3x/wk Some pms	
Marsh			A–C 8–3				
Nelson		J 11–2	A–I 8–3			Weekends	
McArthur			A+B 8–3				Late pms
Neal	A 8:30–5:30					A Sun. Some pms	
Parks	A 8:30–2:30						May take C
Raymond	C 9–12		A+B 8–3	Sometimes	Some pms	A+B wk-ends/eves	
Sedman		A 8–11:30					
Sandle			A 7:30–4:30				
Samuels	A 9–12						Apms
Tilman	A 8:30–4:30					Some on wkends	
Tyler	A 3x/wk 12:30–3:30						
Wyatt	B 9–12		A 8:30–2:30 A 2:30–5 B 12–5			Eves + alt. Sat.	

NOTE: A=eldest child, B=next child, and so forth; am=morning; pm=afternoon; eves=evenings.
SOURCE: Gail Howrigan, Qualifying Paper, Harvard University, 1976.

collaborators Kevin Doughtery, Maureen Durham, Gail Howrigan, Michael Pratt, Michael Schudson, Ronald Thomas, and Heather Weiss.

6. The Families and Communities Project, funded by the Robert Sterling Clark Foundation and the National Institute of Mental Health (Laura Lein, principal investigator) is a study of family social and support networks in one New England community. A systematically selected sample of 120–150 families will be interviewed. In addition, researchers are interviewing personnel at agencies and organizations serving families and communities. This project is currently in progress at the Wellesley College Center for Research on Women.

Lower Middle-Income Families. The twenty-five families participating in the Working Family Project (WFP) were all two-parent families living in the greater Boston area, with both parents employed and with preschoolers present in the home. Family income was between $8,000 and $20,000 a year. This research project was designed to study the child care options chosen by parents in light of several significant structural characteristics of their households. These middle-income families were ineligible for government support of any child care, but none of them possessed sufficient income to hire extensive inside-the-home help such as a housekeeper or *au pair* girl. Some details concerning the demographic characteristics of the families described in the text appear in Table 2–10. Data on the child care arrangement of all WFP families appear in Table 2–11.

Higher-Income Families. A second source of data on child care arrangements is the ongoing Families and Community Project (FCP), which began in the fall of 1977. Building on the WFP, this study focuses on the social networks of families and how these networks are utilized to perform the day-to-day tasks of work and family life, such as child care. The Families and Communities Project extends WFP themes to the middle- to upper-middle-class, two-parent white household. Since the FCP is still in the early stages of data collection, we cannot present tallies of child care strategies for comparison with the WFP tallies. Instead, the child care strategies of five FCP families were selected to illustrate the diversity of child care and employment arrangements found within the middle class and to suggest how the child care options of more affluent households differ from those of more financially constrained families.

The FCP families differ from WFP households in three critical ways. As Table 2–10 indicates, all six FCP households report an annual family income of more than $20,000—a figure higher than the earnings of any WFP family. In addition, FCP families tend to be well educated; most of the husbands and wives have attended, if not completed, college, and four of the five husbands hold advanced degrees. As one might expect, FCP husbands hold high status managerial or professional jobs. In short, compared with the six WFP families, the FCP families are more affluent, better educated, and the husbands hold higher status positions.

3
The Lawyer and the Child

Nathan Glazer

This paper raises a question that may, on the surface, be considered a sideshow in the great issues of child care policy: The growing emphasis on the protection of the child from parents, from teachers, from social workers, from caretakers in general. The scale of this development is such that it is hardly necessary to document it. Almost every issue of a newspaper supplies evidence.

For example, the *Boston Globe* of September 19, 1978, reports, "Suit challenges taking parents from children . . . the welfare department is being challenged on whether it acts too quickly, and without enough investigation, in removing children in care and protection cases from their natural homes and placing them in foster care." This case, brought by the Greater Boston Legal Services Juvenile Law Reform Project, illustrates one issue that is being heavily litigated in many forms. Another type concerns teachers and principals, who have long been under attack for decisions affecting children. In Massachusetts, elected councils in each district have been established under law to protect the rights of children. Each is provided at state cost with a legal advocate. In a case now under way, an advocate is challenging the schools because a child was held back in one grade rather than promoted to another, on grounds of the child's educational difficulties and needs.

In the field of mental retardation, the federal government requires every state receiving federal development disability money to set up— and support—"protection and advocacy systems" independent of the state. Judges, as in the well-known Willowbrook case (*New York State Association for Retarded Children* v. *Carey*),[1] had earlier required an

---

[1] The Willowbrook Development Center, now the Staten Island Development Center, a very large institution for the mentally retarded in New York State,

advocate independent of the parent to protect the independent rights of a mentally retarded child (or adult). These rights require advocate intervention when the child is to be moved to another institution, into a community placement, to a foster home, or even back into his or her own home. The return of the child to his or her own home with the willingness of the parent—as I understand the system established in Willowbrook—would require an intervening advocate to protect the rights of the child as distinct from that of the family.

Of course protection against commitment to an institution for mental illness or mental retardation in the first place is even stronger. The *Washington Post* reported on July 7, 1978, "Children under 18 years old could no longer be committed against their will to St. Elizabeth's Hospital at their parents' request without a full hearing in which they are represented by attorneys according to a general agreement reached here in an attempt to end a four-year-old lawsuit." In this case, attorneys for the Children's Defense Fund brought the suit. In Pennsylvania, the state supreme court has ruled that all children in institutions for mental retardation, public or private, must have hearings as to whether they are properly in these institutions and must be represented by attorneys.

Clearly this is a very mixed bag of examples. The only common feature is that a lawyer—sometimes a lay advocate, but in the nature of the case almost all advocacy eventually involves a professional lawyer—intervenes between some institution, formal or informal, and the child. He may intervene between the parent and the child, when the parent feels that an institutional setting is best or necessary for the child. He may intervene for the parent between the institution and the child. The advocate may intervene because he is summoned into the case by the parent, or he may be summoned by the child. In a case reported September 21, 1978, in the *Boston Globe*, a child of fifteen sought protection from the American Civil Liberties Union against her parents' insistence that she have an abortion.

Often the advocate intervenes on the initiative of neither the child nor the parent but is required by law or court order to play a role, as in the case of mental retardation or mental disabilities. Sometimes, although it may appear that the parent or the child has activated the advocate, he is actually operating independently in order to establish some new principle of child protection and has in effect sought out his plaintiff. Or the lawyer advocate may be seeking to go far beyond the

---

currently operates under a judicial consent decree as the result of a class action undertaken to protect the rights of residents and to change the pattern of treatment they receive.

establishment of principle to establish a new policy approach to a problem.

In the Willowbrook case, the lawyers began with the intention of improving conditions at Willowbrook, under a presumed constitutional right to treatment or to protection from cruel or unusual punishment. They went on to achieve, through consent judgment, commitment by the state to a major program for deinstitutionalizing the retarded.

While the lawyer advocate in such cases must represent plaintiffs in some sense, under class actions he represents all members of a class, even if only some of them accept his advocacy and even if many of them actually reject what he is advocating. In the Willowbrook case, for example, the New York State Association for Retarded Children, which brought the case and for whom the case is still named, ironically dismissed its New York Civil Liberties Union lawyers because it felt they no longer properly represented its interests. Despite this, they are still apparently the leading lawyers in the case. A lawyer can thus represent plaintiffs he has searched out, or clients he has persuaded to allow him to represent them, not for the ends they may have formulated but for the ends of larger policy changes he wishes to institute. Furthermore, he can continue to represent clients who no longer trust him or want him to represent them, and can maintain an independent position against the state and other lawyers representing groups of parents for the retarded. He can also require the state to pay his legal fees, if the judge accepts his intervention as being in the public interest.

This development is important in its own right for issues of child care. Who has the right to decide what arrangements shall be made for a child? Of course this question affects primarily children at the margin —neglected children, juvenile delinquents, or mentally ill or mentally retarded children—for whom some kind of painful decision is faced by parents, by institutions such as juvenile courts, and by police, social workers, and probation officers who come into a situation because a child is neglected or in difficulties. But it is a mistake to underestimate the number of such children.

Further, the principle of advocacy and of lawyerly intervention need not be limited to such cases. In some legal minds there is no reason why the advocate should not protect the normal child and in normal circumstances. John E. Coons and Stephen D. Sugarman, who have written an excellent book arguing that parents should have the first and primary obligation for making decisions for their children, seem to be the strongest defenders of the rights of the family. However, they foresee the possibility that if the parents' decisions are in some sense deemed wrong or inadequate, an agent—some form of advocate for the child—might intervene to make other decisions.[2] A lawyer arguing the need for a lawyer to represent the interests of each mentally retarded child facing institutionalization considers whether parents who place their children in private care must also face a lawyer-protector of the rights of their child. Yes, they must: "If private facilities were excluded . . . one would be opting basically to give persons with money or other forms of influence a greater measure of influence over the rights of others [note that their children have become "others"] than those less fortunate." Further, he wonders whether he should limit required representation only to cases where a child is being institutionalized. "Should military schools or boarding schools for the exceptional child also be included? Perhaps in logic they should. Indeed, opponents of the principle [of required legal representation] can extend this form of argument to parental insistence on one public school as opposed to another, since this involves at least a temporary loss of liberty."[3]

Let us not underestimate the expansive power of the principle of individual rights. If it is damaging to the child to be sent to an institution which purports to care for him, one can at least see the possibility that some lawyer will oppose the right of a young child to be sent into a care situation that does not involve full-time institutionalization and yet one that he considers bad for that child.

Lawyers and Mediating Structures

The relevance of these developments to the concept of mediating structures is, I think, clear, if complex. The argument is that in issues of

---

[2] *Education by Choice: The Case for Family Control* (Berkeley: University of California Press, 1978), p. 67. Peter Skerry pointed out to me that this is a considerable limitation on the principle of family control. The specific quotation is: "Alternatively (or perhaps additionally) [to minimum educational requirements], the state might intervene as it does through the system of family courts that deal with child neglect, that is, by taking up the cases of those relatively few children whose education has been seriously neglected. The initial mechanism for this approach, however, should not be a court; an administrative inspectorate might better be commissioned to challenge the educational assignments. . . . The inspectorate . . . could be given authority to order educational counseling for families found to have violated their responsibility. For more serious cases it could hold a veto power over particular choices. . . . Under certain circumstances it could even be empowered to substitute for the family in selecting the child's educational experience; if necessary, foster parents could be assigned to make the choice." I hasten to add this does not reflect the dominant tone of the book, but it is necessary to point out that even strong supporters of the family's right to choose tend to develop rather baroque forms of child protection.

[3] See Fred Cohen, "Advocacy," in *The Mentally Retarded Citizen and the Law,* Michael Kindred and others, eds. (New York: Free Press, 1976), p. 602.

social policy it is best to devolve responsibility to the small and informal institutions that mediate between the individual and the state. In the first instance, and indeed to as great an extent as possible, the family should be responsible for the child, and this principle is widely accepted in the area of child care—except for difficult and marginal cases. Further, if extrafamilial institutions must be called in, those closest to child and family would be preferred. The model for mediating structures is the ethnic group or the church or the close-knit neighborhood, and from this perspective one would argue that if the family needs assistance in caring for the child—or the child needs assistance in overcoming cruel, incompetent, or neglectful parents—ideally these small-scale institutions should do the job. It is these little brigades, operating on the basis of accepted and informal values, which bind together family, child, and caring institution.

What impact does the intervention of law—or, to be concrete, the lawyer—have in this situation? In many situations, the lawyer intervenes as the protector of the mediating structures principle. He represents parents who do not want their children taken away by welfare agencies; he represents children and parents who prefer a small-scale, familial institution to a large and inevitably formal and distant institution such as Willowbrook. But complexity and ambiguity enter when the institutionalization of legal protection protects the child not only against the large institution, but also against that most intimate of institutions, the family. In the mental retardation protection and advocacy system, a lawyer will play a role in deciding whether the child goes back to the family that wants him or goes into the treatment the family thinks best for him. Further, the child-protection lawyer would not be particularly sympathetic to the mediating structures that might want to take charge of the child in cases of family inadequacy, in cooperation with the family or against the family. First, the lawyer inevitably thinks in terms of universal principles—"equal protection of the law," "due process." These principles are better protected by large and formal institutions than by small, informal ones. They are better protected, for example, in the state university than the denominational college, the public than the private school, and the public school child care setting than the church or family child care setting, and they are the least applicable within the family itself. Second, the child-protection lawyer, coming out of a civil-liberties and civil-rights tradition, tends to be suspicious of particularistic ethnic and religious groups, which would favor dealing with one kind of child rather than another, and would favor educating the child into distinctive values. Third, the child-protection lawyer is disproportionately drawn from an ethnic and religious group that is most committed to universal values, most suspicious of exclusion and particularistic values. I speak of Jews, and of course I speak of a *tendency*—Jews, the most liberal of ethnic-religious groups, are now also prominent among neoconservatives, and of course they have always managed in the modern epoch to combine their universalism with a commitment to the maintenance of distinctive ethno-religious institutions. Finally, the group that has most strongly protected the mediating structures principle, the Catholics, is now somewhat in disarray and is not regarded with much friendliness by public-interest lawyers.

Thus I do not think the child-protection and child-advocacy lawyer will be sympathetic to the ethnic or religious child-care institution that ideally would come into play as mediating structures in cases of family inadequacy. I speak of institutional tendency, rather than of any absolute rule. Of course lawyers can be found on both sides of any case, but I believe the major thrust of the public-interest lawyer and law firm is toward the universal, the public, the formal protection of rights in something akin to full legal process, and large and formal institutions would provide a better home for these interests and commitments than the small and informal ones—including the family itself.

Yet public-interest lawyers and child advocates defend both the family against the state, and the child against the family. They defend children against what is conceived of as the cruelty, indifference, and damage, intended and unintended, of the state, and they insist on the obligation of the state to place children for care or adoption without regard for race or ethnicity. These are mixed objectives, and it would seem that whatever the general ideology or outlook of the public-interest lawyer, as an advocate of the child he is as much on the side of mediating structures as against them. After all, his major enemy *is* the state. He delights in combat with school systems, the child justice system, the social welfare system, the monster institutions for the mentally ill and the mentally retarded. He is, one would think, first and foremost the critic of the big brigades of the state. Despite his doubts about the exclusivist and rights-limiting tendencies of families, churches, ethnic groups, and the like, as a critic of the state and its pretensions, he is doing good and, whether he intends to be or not, is a friend of the mediating structures.

Constraints on State Agencies

The rise of formal children's rights, led by lawyers representing civil rights organizations and by law centers specializing in children's rights, thus creates a paradox. These lawyers have constrained the state and defended the interests of the family in raising its own children the way it wants. But they do not necessarily believe the family is in the best position to know what is right for the child, for they also protect the child against the family. On the basis of an ultimate and absolute individualism, these lawyers reject all forms of organization in which constraint may be imposed. The first is certainly the state; the second is the family itself. And the third, and perhaps most important for the discussion of mediating structures, is the group of institutions in between the family and the state that ideally serve as a protection for the family, even if they sometimes conflict with it.

Individual rights alone do not provide a pattern for the raising of children or for child care. The family, at least in the past and to some extent today, calls out to the church, the ethnic organization, the neighborhood. Since these structures do not have powers of constraint, they are not commonly the target of the child-protection lawyer in his defense of child individualism. The family, undermined as it is by many factors, hopes that the local pastor, the ethnic organization with its attempt at children's activities, or the neighbors who perhaps share some common morality may assist in child-rearing. This assistance may be direct, as when children are left with neighbors or at the local child care centers, or indirect, as when the institutions propound, alongside the family, a common morality and a common set of values.

Like the family, these institutions have been terribly undermined by many factors. The expansion of state functions tells part of the story, along with the rise of mass communications, easy transportation, mass education, and the spread of cosmopolitan values and an individualistically based rights orientation ("due process," "equal protection"). Because this first line of mediating institutions has weakened, the family reaches out to agencies of the state itself for assistance—to the school, which it hopes will discipline, as well as educate and care for the child; to the social welfare agencies, which the family often turns to when the child has some difficulty; even to the police, who in low-income areas traditionally had the function more of exercising and reinforcing family authority and common community morality and values than of fighting crime. These institutions are not regarded as "mediating structures," yet they serve mediating-structure-like functions, insofar as they express the common values, operate through informal modes, and assist the family in achieving its aims for its children.

This may be a surprising view, both to developers of mediating structures theory and to the advocates of child protection, who commonly see school, social worker, and police as enemies, to be limited and constrained in their value-expressive and disciplinary functions.

Nevertheless, such agencies of the state do function as mediating structures with some support from family and local, nonstate institutions. The lawyer monitors and limits the work of all these state agencies, in particular those functions which are informal and value-expressive. Of course the policeman can still arrest the child, but he finds it more difficult to express his own concept of proper behavior and exert an informal and familial-like discipline. Of course the social worker may still provide services, but the kinds of services he may provide are increasingly hemmed in by rules and regulations defending the rights of the child. The juvenile court still has great power, but it must constrain its informality; the teacher can still teach, but he cannot express the common morality by disciplining a child, either through harsh words or physical punishment. Having stated all this, let me defend myself and say that I am *not* advocating police harassment short of arrest, removing children from adequate homes at the discretion of social workers and juvenile judges, or allowing teachers to ridicule or beat students. However, I am merely describing how public agencies with a mediating structures role, have been stripped of their informal value-inducing and disciplinary functions by the elaborate development of rights and the processes that protect them. And I am recalling that these agencies did possess these functions and that the family commonly saw them as allies rather than as enemies.

The evils of religion, the church, and the organized ethnic group (as well as the repressive family) were exposed some time ago. These structures are by now so weakened that we look upon them with a certain nostalgic sympathy and try to resurrect what they once seemed to do. We have moved on to a situation in which the evils of all state agencies and agents—social work, the social worker, the juvenile court, the probation officer, the police, the school, the teacher, and the educational bureaucracy—are being fully exposed and properly hemmed in by the one profession that still seems to retain its glamour and reputation for purity of motive, the civil rights lawyer. Not only does current research reveal the inadequacy of these agencies and agents, but historical research has revealed the worm in the apple, illicit motives behind the fine language that created the child care systems. As many historians have told us, the Protestants wanted to convert the Catholics, and the Catholics in response walled out the modern world; the white Anglo-Saxons wanted to suppress the cultures of the immigrants; the upper and middle classes wanted to produce docile labor from rebellious youth; and all were expressing their puritan horror of immigrant and Catholic attitudes to drink, sex, and fun on Sunday. And yet, little things break through the accounts to convince me this revisionist phase in the history and analysis of child-care agencies is overdrawn. Reading between the lines—and even along the lines—one discovers that immigrant parents often supported the activities of Protestant and Anglo-Saxon child care agencies, not only the schools, but often all the specifically disciplinary institutions. Many of those working in these institutions were not puritan bigots or sadists but caring and concerned people who could reach across cultural and religious barriers and who more often than the more exaggerated revisionism suggests were drawn from varied ethnic and religious groups themselves. One of the best of the revisionist accounts of the juvenile justice institutions, Steven L. Schlossman's *Love and the American Delinquent*, demonstrates that the personnel of one institution, the juvenile court, now considered a prime example of the repressiveness of unsuitable informality in treatment of children, was of varied social, ethnic, and religious background very early in its history.[4]

Schlossman's description of the first superintendent of the Wisconsin Reform School, a Victorian who believed in the power of affection, family life, and proper environment for the rearing of young boys, suggests how much of the mediating structure could be incorporated into a state institution. Moses Barrett was indifferent to the reasons for a boy's incarceration, whether family neglect or criminal acts. All could be properly reared through the proper environment.

> He vowed to incorporate a "family spirit" in the reformatory by his daily labors. Central to this effort were his wife and teen-age daughters, who served respectively as matron and teachers. Through them Barrett hoped to recreate the moral presence of a righteous middle-class family. Every evening he would bring inmates, his wife, and daughters together for what he termed a "family" conference, combining prayer, confession, ethical instruction, and, most importantly, sympathetic listening.[5]

Aside from the question of the effectiveness of this kind of institution, it would be interesting to see how this kind of approach could survive in a present-day state-aided institution. Obviously prayer would have to go. So undoubtedly would confession—no boy could be allowed to testify against himself. The family could not participate unless it had credentials. And would the social workers union allow Barrett to spend so much time at his job?

In other words, within the concept of mediating structures certain

---

[4] (Chicago: University of Chicago Press, 1977), pp. 145–147.
[5] Schlossman, *Love and the American Delinquent*, p. 97.

functions are seen as important in society: inculcation of values, a caring and concerned attitude, maintenance of distinctive culture and ethical traditions, social structures in which people are involved and effective. I suggest that some of these functions have been taken over by the state agencies that are the primary target of the child-rights movement, and as a result these functions have been damaged. I referred earlier to a Boston suit in which the welfare department was charged with taking children from their parents too precipitately. The suit followed on the heels of a scandal in which a child under the department's protection had been allowed to stay with parents and was subsequently killed through neglect and cruelty. This is more than a case of "damned if you do, and damned if you don't," of making difficult choices and not always the right one (though it is that, too, of course). But attacks on the welfare department—on what a rights-oriented lawyer sees as abuses which his litigating skills and subsequent legal reforms could eliminate—are attacks on the discretion of the welfare workers and on their ability to take up roles in defense of the family and the child. The assumption is that a new legal rule can solve the problem. But I would argue that in difficult situations in which someone's discretion must be employed, the legal rule can merely reduce the range of discretion and so reduce the range of responsibility, concern, and care.

In responsibility begins effectiveness. If one does not have discretion then one applies the rules mechanically and knows one is safe. Just as this is no way to raise a child, it is no way to protect a child, but it is exactly what the legalistic child-protection approach must lead to.[6]

Child Care Settings

What bearing does the grim frontier of child abuse and child incarceration have on the more general issues of child care? Child care outside the family is an inevitable function in a society in which increasing numbers of mothers want to or must work and in which some kind of communal arrangement for the care of children is necessary. Many people would agree that for the care of the child the next best thing to the family—some would argue even better than the contemporary family in some respects—are settings that reproduce in large measure the family. They should be small. They should not be rule bound. They should express distinctive values and culture not markedly discontinuous with that of the family itself (there may be argument about this, but I would defend this as a legitimate concern of the family). In some cases,

---

[6] See Harry L. Miller, "The 'Right to Treatment': Can the Courts Rehabilitate and Cure?" *Public Interest*, no. 46 (Winter 1977), pp. 96–118.

they should assist in the development of those values which the family feels it cannot effectively inculcate. One can well imagine families who would like a traditional religious or cultural setting for their children because they cannot well provide one themselves. Other families might want the child care setting to support academic and intellectual values which they cannot provide.

All these objectives can best be served in distinctive institutions, doing what they believe in and hiring staff, trained and untrained, that best support what they want to do. The rules can be variable, but they must be rules that parents are comfortable with and that the parent-surrogates also find reasonable and natural. The mothers of children should have the freedom and opportunity to make use of such institutions. But I do not think we can provide this opportunity in settings directly organized by the state, whether through the educational or social service systems.

There are good reasons for this, and bad reasons, and what seemed good at one time may seem bad with time and experience. The good reasons are the separation of church and state, the public commitment against segregation and for integration, the development of civil service rules and protection for state employees, the protections against improper use of state funds and fraud, and the rise of various forms of child protection in law and regulation that make the parent-surrogate behave very differently from the parent, even if and when the parent would want the surrogate to act like a parent. Under these circumstances, I would favor child care settings closer to the family, in space and style, and public mechanisms that would assist in creating such settings—not the direct creation of child care centers by public authorities but state support by means of something like vouchers. With the present development of legal doctrine, however, I wonder whether any kind of public support can coexist with the style and character of a mediating institution and not inevitably blight it.

Child-protection law, most applicable in public centers, introduces formal rules for the protection of the individual into situations where informality and discretion should prevail and where the individual is still in process of being formed by social setting. Clearly, this has happened for good and sufficient reasons. Many agents with discretion abused it, they became smug and self-confident in their professional knowledge; following their own values they infringed on the discretion and choice of others and used their freedom from legal procedures to prevail over the family and small groups. But what path can we take to resuscitate family-based discretion and values, particularly when we must call on agents and agencies that are funded by a rule-bound state?

Obviously I have given only a general perspective, and ahead is the hard work of arguing about the specific rules that govern state funds when they are used for the infinitely complex and varied task of caring for children. But since I began with the lawyers, I will end with them. David Rothman has put together an interesting book on the distrust of benevolence, which is now so widespread and is at the root of lawyerly power and rule expansion. In this book a psychoanalyst, Willard Gaylin, emphasizes that the relation of mother and child contains a fund of love and benevolence that we must consider the primary base of child care. A lawyer, Ira Glasser, emphasizes how abusive of children's rights the state has been and how it must be constrained (while this is no major part of his contribution, inevitably he must also want to constrain the family when it transgresses what he conceives to be children's constitutionally protected rights). Rothman, moderating between the antagonists, writes: "It was Willard Gaylin who commented, with all sarcasm intended, that he finally understood the motive impulse of the adversarial movement: to substitute for the hard-nosed, belligerent, and tough-minded psychiatrist the attention of the gentle, understanding, empathetic lawyer!"[7] The point is not that we must reestablish the all-knowing psychoanalyst and his lesser brood of semiprofessional child care experts in place of the child-protection lawyer. But if we have now become aware of the limits of the professional knowledge and claims of the child care professional, let us not substitute for our lost illusions an exaggerated faith in what the law and lawyers can do for our children.

---

[7] Willard Gaylin, Ira Glasser, Steven Marcus, and David Rothman, *Doing Good: The Limits of Benevolence* (New York: Pantheon, 1978), p. 94.

4
Report on the Conference

Sidney Callahan

Most discussions of the family and child care are alike; in a very short time existing differences of opinion surface and are fought over or politely avoided. Perhaps such conflict is inevitable, since everyone was once a child and on becoming an adult has faced serious decisions concerning family matters. If personal emotional commitments influence ordinary people in their discussions of the family, one can imagine the potential for heated disagreements among highly competent persons who work in the field professionally.

Such a group attended the two-day conference of the Mediating Structures Project initiated by Peter Berger and Richard Neuhaus. Among the gathering were those who have studied and written on the family and child care institutions, those who have provided therapeutic interventions in and out of institutional contexts, and those who have been involved in policy discussions of the family, both in and out of government. In no way did this group politely avoid conflict.

In fact keeping order among these thirty-five or so highly articulate people at one big table, in a medium-sized room for two days was no small accomplishment. Peter Berger and Richard Neuhaus did an admirable job as they took turns chairing the sessions; in addition they were called upon to explain and expand on the concept of their Mediating Structures Project. What counts as a mediating structure? Is the Supreme Court, for instance, a mediating structure? As the published description makes clear, mediating structures are "those institutions standing between the individual in his private life and the large institutions of public life."[1] Some face-to-face interaction is implied which

---

[1] Peter L. Berger and Richard John Neuhaus, *To Empower People: The Role of Mediating Structures in Public Policy* (Washington, D.C.: American Enterprise Institute, 1977).

would rule out the Supreme Court. Such large and distant institutions are called "megastructures" and are seen as the source of alienation and powerlessness in modern American society. Mediating structures, on the other hand, consist of institutions such as the family, church, neighborhood, and voluntary association that mediate between the purely private and impersonal public spheres: "Such institutions have a private face, giving private life a measure of stability, and they have a public face, transferring meaning and value to the megastructures." Berger and Neuhaus propose that mediating structures should "be more imaginatively recognized in public policy," so that "individuals would be more 'at home' in society, and the political order would be more 'meaningful.' " Indeed, in their view democracy depends on such vital voluntary associations to serve as a defense against totalitarianism. The point of a conference on the family as a child care institution, one in a series on the various mediating structures, is to explore ways that the mediating structure of the family can be protected and fostered by public policy.

The conference began with Brigitte Berger's paper presenting the concept of mediating structures in relation to child care. That afternoon Dr. Dale Meers, a psychologist from Washington, D.C., reported on his research with one inner city population. He emphasized with clinical detail the incredible environmental stress and pressure on the children and families in his sample. The next morning Mary Jo Bane gave a presentation on existing patterns of services for children; and in the afternoon of the second day Nathan Glazer focused on the particular case of the relationship of the lawyer and the child in public policy. On each day of the conference the formal presentations encompassed both empirical research data and larger policy discussions. In between, around and about, there flowed in the disorganized way of all conferences a rushing and meandering stream of arguments, statements, counterarguments, counterstatements, comments, questions, examples, and counterexamples. In her opening remarks Brigitte Berger had said she wished to emphasize differences in the varying approaches to the family—and she was successful. Sharp differences were produced.

In the ongoing and sometimes repetitiously circular flow, three large arenas of disagreement could be discerned and delineated. The most basic but most subtle disagreements concerned the priority of ideals and values which should govern family life and child care. Along with conflicts over basic assumptions about what ought to be positively valued, there were differences apparent in what people feared, dreaded, and considered most harmful. The second large arena of disagreement was less subtle and implicit than the first and involved empirical ques-

69

tions: What is actually happening now and what happened in the past? Which empirical facts, whose experiences, judgments, and data count? Naturally these arguments and differences over facts often seemed somewhat related to the implicit values of the participants, despite the accumulated years of training in intellectual objectivity.

The third arena of conflict and argument follows logically if not sequentially from the first two: What should be done in future public policy decisions concerning the family and child care? Which efforts should be made at what costs? What should be left undone to avoid harmful side effects? A brief overview of these three fronts of the battle will be given, with only the sparest identification of combatants and skirmishes.

Conflicting Values for Families and Child Care

One of the first conflicts of the conference arose over the possibility of defining what constitutes a "good family" or "good home." Brigitte Berger in her presentation and paper argued that no one knows what produces good outcomes in child-rearing; all past research efforts to predict the future of certain child-rearing practices and home conditions have been fruitless. Moreover, professional child-rearing advice has fluctuated so much over the years that any efforts to say that today's experts and professionals know better than ordinary parents must be suspect. Parents should never be intimidated by or subjected to efforts calculated to "professionalize" parenthood. Intrusions should be kept to a minimum, and professional interventions that are deemed necessary generally should be viewed as ancillary rather than adversary to the family.

A parent is defined by Brigitte Berger as anyone who is willing to take complete responsibility for a child over a long time. Since parents as opposed to professional experts love their own children, they are the ones who will be most likely to make the best decisions concerning their children, on the basis of such a complete and long-range commitment. The positive ideal and value here is one of autonomous functioning families caring for themselves and creatively solving their own problems in a multitude of equally good ways. Parental privacy, pluralism, and heterogeneity is highly valued.

Many participants at the conference endorsed Brigitte Berger's view of the positive value of diversity and autonomy. Supporting comments were forthcoming. It was pointed out that black families may have different child-rearing practices from others in the society, and fundamentalists may have intensely religious values not shared by the

70

majority of Americans. No one can have enough knowledge to label different child-rearing traditions "abusive" or neglectful. Often more informal arrangements for child care may be of higher quality than formal or professionally organized systems. Nor can cross-cultural comparisons of other child care systems throw much light on the heterogeneous American scene. In our diverse situation parents must be able to pass their own distinct values to their children by being empowered to decide and choose what they think best. In almost all conflicts of interest parents should be given first priority.

Fears and aversions accompanying this positive value stance were also voiced vigorously by both Brigitte Berger and others present. One worry is that professionals will wrongfully demoralize and override parents' own better judgments about their children. This cultural and psychological imperialism can produce self-distrust and denigration of one's own particular tradition in the name of universalism and modernization. As the influence of professionals grows homogenization takes place, and the pluralism and particularity that make American democracy great will be eroded. Even the new so-called champions of the family with their agitation for a national family policy may be dangerous.

Worse still, the fear is that bureaucrats and professionals who need clients in order to keep their jobs will intrude more and more on the rights and freedom of parents. Children can be removed from "abusive" parents and be lost forever in child care systems which are harmful to them and their families. Mothers may be forced to go to work and not allowed to stay home with their children. The poor in particular will be the victims of the new class of professional experts who impose their own standards and guard their own bureaucratic sources of money and power through coercion of parents. In addition, the economic costs of supporting these destructive professional institutions and services will be enormous and borne by those who can least afford to pay. The family will suffer if the family's welfare is used as a screen or tool by those who really wish to effect larger social reforms such as redistribution of income. To help the family one must keep the focus on the family and empower the choices of parents.

This picture of the family and the general approach presented by Brigitte Berger and supported by others present did not go unchallenged. Most of the challenges were made in the empirical arena, but there were some basic conflicts over ideals and values. Dr. Dale Meers made the point that while one may not be able to define good families or a good home, it is possible to define harmful family practices. Pathology does exist. A parental choice, for instance, to separate a child from its love object too early and for too long, as in many extended families or in day care situations, can result in long-term damage which does not show up until much later stages of individual development. Parents may adhere to their particular ethnic practices or to their national day care arrangements and inflict damage on their children.

Others also agreed that at least bad homes can be defined, and parents may choose to act so harmfully that intervention may be mandated if one takes the right of the individual child as a primary value. The mediating structures concept of family could itself be seen as an effort to impose one model and ideal of family upon others—a model that overstresses the rights of parents and the family group. Should the individual exist for the family or does the family exist for the individual? When choosing between the parents' rights, a child's rights, or an individual woman's right to work, why should the parents' claims be given priority? Sheila Kammerman from her perspective as an expert on child care argued that the rights of the individual should be given priority.

It seemed that those who tended to adhere to what Nathan Glazer in his paper calls liberal universal values could not give up the primary ideal of individual equality to see children's rights or women's rights subordinated to parental rights or the welfare of the family as a whole. The universal approach, heir to the Enlightenment, also stresses rationality, scientific progress, and objectivity. Thus professionals may know more than parents, and many parents may desire to professionalize parenthood as a positive gain. Alfred Kahn in his comments often defended the values of equality, justice, and rational intervention on different scales. He maintained, too, that cross-cultural studies of child care systems can serve as natural experiments from which much can be learned that can be helpful for American society. Reason, research, and science make life better, as when babies do not die of malnutrition or disease. In the same vein, law, bureaucracies, and programs run by professionals may be effectively and sensitively run to meet diverse needs.

The fear implicit in the liberal universal approach to family and child care is of a new suppression of individual rights and equality. The child's rights may be endangered if parents are empowered even more than they already are. Women now have to work, and their equality may be endangered if there are no available child care institutions. In the return to family rights and an emphasis upon informal private arrangements, there lies the danger of a new laissez-faire policy of neglect, which as always will favor the strong over the weak.

72

Arguments over Empirical Questions

Arguments over what is and what has been the case in family and child care matters were also vigorously pursued during the conference. Personal implicit values seemed to shape these accounts of empirical data, just as the particular experiences of individuals form their values and shape their ideals. Whether one has seen more abused children or more poor abused, powerless parents may make a difference. Furthermore, the choice of research subject and the manner in which research questions are shaped may be similarly influenced by personal experiences. Unfortunately, in a domain as encompassing as family, child care, and public policy, both a lack of data and a plethora of data produce an ambiguity which can be variously interpreted. Empirical arguments turned repeatedly to the effects of intervention, the role of policy, the role of professionals, and the state of child care institutions and arrangements.

Perhaps the most basic disagreements concerned the role of government and professional intervention. Is it the case that outside aid has damaged older self-regulating systems in which the family could take care of its own? Are blacks in the ghetto the victims of racism, unemployment, crime, malnutrition, and inadequate schools, police, and health clinics as Dr. Meers suggested? Or, as Richard Neuhaus proposed, are black communities also suffering, in addition to racism and poverty, from being victims of professionally run bureaucracies that ignore real needs and intrude destructively? Can it be the case, suggested others, that welfare does harm the family by destroying initiative and the need for husband and wife to stay together? Or as Robert Hill pointed out, is it the professional researchers who are framing the question incorrectly? They focus on the failures when there are statistically more successes.

Other arguments over the effects of intervention involved the question of licensure and state regulations. Do such state requirements for child care institutions infringe on parental choice, and do such measures often force the shutdown of effective private institutions? Robert Woodson brought up the example of effective private nursing homes that were forced to close because they could not meet standards which the state subsequently ignored in its own substandard institutions. Other cases given were of day care arrangements which satisfied parents, but perhaps because they involved relatives or were too religiously oriented could not be legitimized under state regulations. The counterargument to these cases was to point out that often informal grass-roots organizations could get started only with outside government funding. In any event, once informal voluntary arrangements become successful, inevitably they too become formalized, regulated, and part of the institutional structures, if not a megastructure. What once was left to discretion and informal mechanisms becomes a matter of law and policy when with success and increased size more complicated questions arise.

Another conference argument along these lines was whether establishing policy and rules in institutions harmed or hurt those being served. Nathan Glazer maintained that, in the past, juvenile and family courts, child care agencies, and the local policemen could do a better job when they were given more freedom and discretion. Everybody does his work less well when he must abide by fixed rules and justify each action in fear of being sued by civil rights lawyers. In this controversy, some people pointed out the enhanced protection of rules, policies, and civil rights procedures, while others noted their hampering effects. Horrible examples were cited on both sides of the debate.

Those who run child-service institutions were defended by Pastor Robert Gutheil from the charge of lacking concern for parental and family rights. Often it is other relatives in the family who request that a child be rescued from abuse, and often too it is relatives who offer to foster a child. All foster care is seen as temporary, and attempts are made to reunite families as soon as possible. Still, child abuse does exist as a serious and mounting problem, and resources are needed to deal with it. One of the tragedies from the perspective of those on the front lines is the lack of funding for preventive work, which could help families before breakdowns and crises occur.

Another problem mentioned by Sister Constance Gaynor is that the religious group that founded a voluntary agency may not be willing to continue funding a service when the clients are no longer members of its own particular group. Subsequent comments brought up the fact that religious voluntary agencies and institutions have other dilemmas as well; for example, to avoid pressures public agencies often turn over politically controversial tasks to the voluntary agency. Perhaps even more difficult to deal with is the question of professionalization of staff in the religious institutions. If there is open hiring and everyone must be similarly trained and have developed the same professional expertise, can the particular values and ideals of the religious founders remain? What is the good of being different if an institution no longer has any real distinction?

Again and again the question of the role of professionals emerged. Very different estimates of professionals were given by this group of elite professionals. Are most professionals members of the new class, who now find themselves without clients and so must find new groups for tutelage? Has there historically been a succession of professionals in the field of child care who have displaced each other in waves? Peggy Steinfels, speaking as a historian, reminded the group of the history of social welfare movements in this country. She suggested that just as the social workers displaced the religious volunteers, they may now be being displaced by the public-interest lawyers. If, as was several times suggested, the drive for setting up day care in the public schools was an effort to save the jobs of the excess teachers, so too the unemployed social workers and the excess number of graduating lawyers are precipitating new assaults upon the family's autonomy in the name of children's rights. There seemed to be no sure consensus among the cynics whether the professionals themselves are fully aware of their strategies or simply misguided.

Others thought the cynical view of professionals unfounded and defended professionals as people meeting real and not created needs. The idea of child care professionals threatening the family in some conspiracy seemed a fantasy. Sidney Johnson also thought Brigitte Berger's characterization of the "family champions" unfair. His group, the Family Impact Seminar, has never advocated any monolithic policy but instead always emphasized the variety of families in the United States. Along the way Kenneth Keniston and the Carnegie Council on Children were also defended against the charge of using the family as a tool of social reform. Those who see family welfare as being tied in with income distribution do so because they think that is what it will take to solve the family's main problem—poverty and lack of jobs and money. Child care allowances and vouchers would not be adequate help for families caught in the larger economic forces of the society. Peggy Steinfels spoke to this point when she described the immigrant Irish in New York who suffered from as much addiction and disorganization as any families today and could not change the situation without changing employment patterns.

Steinfels used another historical analogy to make a point regarding families versus professionals. As in the nineteenth century, families today often actively manipulate professionals and the service institutions to get what they want and need. Many others agreed that families are not passive recipients or helpless victims of aid but also shapers of the system; they are inventive and innovative in meeting problems. In fact, some noted, the use of civil rights lawyers by parents as in the Willowbrook case has been one move to use professionals to control other professionals for the sake of children in the family. Parents of handicapped children may be most vulnerable to the coercion of the expert professional, but if they do not succumb they may also be the most creative and active parents. The family's role in caring for handicapped children should be emphasized, a point made strongly by Brigitte Berger and seconded by Dr. Luitgard Wundheiler.

Normal children and ordinary child care was the focus of Mary Jo Bane's paper, but once again there were arguments over the weighting of ambiguous data. At least everyone agreed that families creatively put together packages of different kinds of child care arrangements to fulfill their needs. Descriptions of these packaging arrangements in Bane's paper were supplemented by Sheila Kammerman's report of her research on working mothers. Parents often use combinations of formal and informal arrangements, which are also paid for in different ways, including cash transactions that are unrecorded for tax purposes. It was also generally agreed that parents and others often do not differentiate between nursery school, day care, and Head Start programs.

Disagreements arose over the meaning and import of the data. Can one tell what parents want by looking at what they actually do? Do they want what it is only possible to have? How great a difference does the age of the child make? Are most people happy to have three-year-old children experience some group care, or are many people ambivalent about peer influence for their children? The effects of day care on children's development were debated, along with considerations of whether day care affected the rest of society. Would people prefer home care and to have relatives taking care of their children? Is there any way to have quality institutions which can maintain the diversity and variety of the heterogeneous population? Coercion was seen both in providing and in not providing day care. The lack of day care effectively coerces the working mother's actions, whereas the sheer existence of an available program may also effectively coerce.

Often the debate turned on the nature of the schools as child care institutions. Are they as decentralized as any American institution, or are they coercive, unresponsive examples of everything one would fear in a day care system? James Levine maintained that it was inappropriate to think of the schools as a model for any day care provisions. The most likely model would be closer to the diversified community-run Head Start programs. Either/or aspects of the discussion were not helpful in dealing with child care issues. Of course the questions of costs and funding were also debated, as they were in almost every other issue that came up at the conference.

Public Policy for the Future

Many of the arguments over what should be done as a matter of public policy to aid families followed from the group's disagreements over values and the assessment of empirical data. Those who see family pathology, child abuse, and desperate need as being rare naturally opt for a public policy based on the normal family, which already functions well and should not suffer intrusion. Marginal cases should not affect the larger policy picture. Parents, especially poor powerless parents, should be trusted to know what is best for their children and be empowered to get it with the least intervention and pressure toward conformity. Vouchers and child care allowances will empower parental choice. Not only should policy makers learn from the successful families, but research should be focused on the success to inform future funding decisions. Any intervention should be at the appropriate level and guided by what families want. One first relies on parents, then extended families, then neighborhood, church groups, and voluntary agencies. Always to be avoided are solutions involving large, inefficient bureaucracies that enforce bland homogenization and rigid rules and thereby destructively reduce initiative and discretion of parents, professionals, and children who get caught in the system. The imperialism of professionals also has to be vigorously curbed.

Those conference participants who saw the problems and needs of distressed women, children, and families to be more than marginal could not accept relying on support channeled only through mediating structures and parents. When they weighed the trade-offs involved in the various options and choices, they felt that provisions for child care should have more government support in all the diverse forms that support can take. Nor should the focus be on the family alone. For those who adhere to liberal universal values the plight of individual families, women, and children cannot be separated from some basic income redistribution through provision of jobs, income assistance, or other methods. The rights and needs of the individual child or of the individual woman caught in larger economic forces cry for more than the empowerment of parents, families, or the encouragement of diversity and heterogeneity.

Bertram Beck voiced some reservations about the mediating structures approach to policy. How can we support natural structures without making those structures unnatural? How can we pay relatives when collusion is always a problem in public funding and when relatives are supposed to volunteer in their role as family members? Since what may be good for individuals in the family may not be good for the family structure as a whole, how can we avoid broader issues of redistribution of income? In the end poverty is the real enemy. Others present also argued these points, and while everyone agreed on the pathology of bureaucracies some still felt it is the only way to meet problems as rational persons and citizens desiring justice for all. People in a democracy can shape and control responsive institutions and legislation.

One creative suggestion for effecting change in the central role of professionals was offered by Audrey Cohen. She agreed that professionals are often inhumane and harmful to the development of autonomy on the part of their clients, but this is not inevitable. Professionals can be trained and humanely educated to encourage client independence and discourage client dependence. Successful intervention should be seen as empowering clients with new skills of their own so that they no longer need the assistance of professionals or of the institution. Such procedures could be effective if policy makers could build in new client evaluation procedures of professionals which reward those who educate clients for self-sufficiency. A new reward structure built on new educational measures could help obtain the goal of autonomous families who no longer have to suffer tutelage and intrusion in their lives.

Another important policy consideration for all future measures is the institution of financial accountability. Michael Szenberg, an economist, frequently stressed that one must always count the costs and understand that nothing is ever free. All programs cost money, and who will pay in what tender? Choices have to be made since no society is wealthy enough to afford everything. Differences in scale and economies of scale must be taken into account, and economic trade-offs and compromises made. Certain economic and political forces can be seen as determining and reducing available choices; these forces must be foreseen and taken into consideration. For instance, simply increasing information about available programs will increase participation and the costs involved. In every proposed change there should be built-in accountability. No one should be able to spend money in an institution without knowing where it comes from, having some responsibility for raising it, and accounting for its use to others. Since nothing is really free, it should not be allowed to appear so.

Summary and Comment

This lively two-day debate over public policy confronted perennially problematic questions. How much can we trust individual parents to do what is good for their children? How much can we trust institutions and government actions to solve social problems? Can we trust anyone to decide what is good and what is pathological in child-rearing? Even if these questions could be solved, what could create jobs in this society here and now, and what would it cost? How can we intervene with the least harm?

In my view there are problems in the basic assumptions and ideals of the mediating structures concept, but few objections to the policy recommendations (a view taken by others at the conference). In contrast to Brigitte Berger's optism about parents and pessimism about professionals and institutions, I would take a pessimistic view of both. I think that parents may not know best and that parental love, when it exists, may be able to cloud judgment as well as enhance it. More dangerously, love and hate are closely aligned, and there are inherent conflicts of interest between parents and children. Professionals may be just as likely to know better than parents and intervene for the best interests of the child.

I also think certain ethnic and religious child-rearing practices are abusive, for child abuse exists, can be defined, and is probably more widespread than supposed.

As an unreconstructed adherent of liberal universal values, I would see the family existing for the individual and the larger group, not the individual for the family. Therefore in a conflict of interest I would be sympathetic to children's rights or an individual woman's rights over the family's rights. In fact, the family is so embedded in the larger community through language and economic and cultural values that it is hard to analyze or treat as an autonomous structure. Today's family seems much like a Stone Age family, firmly embedded and dependent upon the tribe as a whole. Ultimately, one cannot help the individual family without changing the whole tribe, or in our case effecting some form of general income redistribution.

But as we know all too well, power in the collective may be even more corrupting than in individuals, parents, or families. The tribe, community, or state should not be inherently trusted any more than parents. Once again the classic American strategy of checks and balances on power is called for, in family policy as in any other domain. Mistrusting and suspicious of power—whether that of parents, professionals, institutions, bureaucracies, or megastructures—one works to distribute power. With the proper distribution of power all will be constrained but still have enough power to function for the good of the individual and group.

Parents' rights have to be respected, not so much because they know best (they may not), or love their children (they may not), or because the family as a whole is more important than the individual (it is not), but because parents cannot function for the good of the individual without power. Parental responsibility cannot be separated from parental power and control either ethically or psychologically. If parents are to be held responsible and continue to carry out the arduous tasks of child-rearing, then they must be given power and discretion. To act effectively the individual's locus of control must be internal, not external; to protect a child a parent needs to be active, not passive, emotionally involved, not detached. External overt intrusions of power should be kept at a minimum and used sparingly. By now we all would agree that there are no viable alternatives to the family as an institution for rearing children.

In empowering families any positive forces for change which may reside within a heterogeneous group of families can also be protected. If families are active innovative institutions (which I doubt, but hope to be true), they must retain enough power in their particularity to survive and influence the larger community. Within limits, letting a thousand families bloom may be best for individuals therein and the society as a whole. But there is a hard-to-define limit to nonintervention. And there will be innumerable arguments over the best ways to widen choice and reduce coercion. Practical arguments will be rooted in the continuing arguments over the ultimate governing values.

As a means of distributing power the mediating structures concept for families is a creative option that should be taken very seriously. Two days was not long enough to begin properly to confront these ideas. Surely these papers and this conference can best be seen as the beginning of a national debate which will affect us all.

5
Retrospective on the Conference

Brigitte Berger

The purpose of the conference was to explore the idea that the family should be the primary agent in child care, in the context of the mediating structures concept. For this reason people with quite different viewpoints were invited; that is, there was no attempt to "pack" the conference. My own paper clearly (and intentionally) served as the foil for much of the controversy. For this reason, as well as because of the evident fact that my own viewpoint and understanding of the import of the conference differs from that of my co-editor, I will take the liberty of making some concluding observations.

The discussion quickly brought to the fore two overall positions, both frequently adhered to with deep conviction. There are those who, with whatever reservations, are positively inclined toward out-of-family child care under professional auspices; and there are those who, with whatever stipulations toward such programs, are inclined to be suspicious of them. Neither group is dispassionate; both have vested interests in the matter, be the interests practical or philosophical. (And I may add that I would not for one moment exclude myself from this characterization.) Not surprisingly, individuals with professional expertise in child care tend to be in the first group, no matter whether this expertise is exercised in practice or in research activities. Those with an overall disposition in favor of large government programs are also likely to be found in this group (I cannot pursue here the interesting correlation between faith in the professions and faith in New Deal–type public delivery of social services). The second group, again not surprisingly, tends to include people with an ideological interest in propagating the family (I definitely belong under this category). Perhaps slightly more surprising was the fact that the three black participants at the conference as well as those with experience in the Hispanic community gave emphatic support to the second position.

The discussion was accordingly heated, especially in the beginning. It is all the more interesting that, toward the end and despite continuing disagreements on both facts and assumptions, there was not much disagreement on the *policy* theses of my paper. Two conclusions could be drawn from this. One would be that these theses are truisms, fatuous enough to command general consensus; the other would be that the theses are indeed irenic, capable of bringing together people approaching the issue from divergent points of departure. Obviously I hope the latter conclusion is correct. This conclusion would also support the general purpose of the Mediating Structures Project, which seeks precisely to offer policy proposals that cut across ideological and political divides.

The strongest opposition to my position came from Alfred Kahn and Sheila Kammerman, on the basis of their own and other research data. The importance of these data may be stipulated. The problem comes with the interpretation of these data, especially the assessment of future trends and policy implications. The data show clearly the increasing number of women with small children entering the labor force and the increasing use of all kinds of day care programs. These trends can be interpreted as continuing into the future and as necessitating an increase in publicly funded out-of-family programs. I think that this interpretation is, at best, doubtful. Class and ethnic factors are crucial here. If such factors are taken into account, it appears that the increase in day care use is largely among white middle-class parents.[1] Working-class families, especially black and Hispanic ones, have different patterns.[2] They use formal day care programs much less, preferring in-home care by members of the extended family or various voluntary and informal neighborhood arrangements, all nonprofessional in character. These facts, of course, could simply be seen as reflecting makeshift responses in the absence of better (that is, out-of-family, professional) alternatives. The data indicate, however, that there are also different attitudes—which were in fact strongly voiced by the black participants, Robert Hill among them.

Those who agree with Kahn and Kammerman will argue that these patterns will shift once programs of another kind are more available. This may well be so. As Leslie Lenkowsky put it well in the discussion,

[1] See Thomas Rodes and John Moore, *National Child Care Consumer Study* (Washington, D.C.: Office of Child Development, 1975).

[2] See Laura Lein, *Working Family Project: Preliminary Report* (Washington, D.C.: National Institute of Education, 1974), as well as the data accumulated by Robert Hill of the National Urban League; a detailed analysis of this material is being done by Peter Skerry as part of the Mediating Structures Project).

free programs are always oversubscribed. But this does not tell us what people would really prefer and what they would do if more options were available. By analogy, if the only restaurant in my neighborhood is vegetarian, I am likely to go there when I am eating out—and I would be likely to eat out often if the food there were free. This says nothing, however, about my desire for steak or about my behavior if a steak house were available to me.

The question of values is central here; to wit, the values of those for whom the proponents of the different positions claim to speak. I insist that the values of ordinary men and women must be taken with utmost seriousness, and that such respect is intrinsic to the democratic ideal. My main concern at the conference was not to promote my own frankly familistic values, but rather to suggest that public policy in this area must be guided by the values of those it is intended to serve. Thus I have no quarrel with those who want their children to have the sort of day care advocated by the liberal professional establishment. But I insist that public policy should be designed to give the widest possible choice for everyone.

This is not at all a reactionary (or even neoconservative) attitude of hostility to the public funding of child care. On the contrary, I believe that such public funding is necessary and will become increasingly necessary. The question is, What kind of programs will be funded?

Nor is there an antiprofessional bias in my position. But the preference of parents over professionals as the chief agents of child care is based on simple considerations that can be put in the form of a want ad: Wanted: A professional expert in child care who will commit himself/herself for at least fourteen years of consistent, uninterrupted care to one group of children; the commitment continues regardless of pay or the absence of payment; no fixed hours, no sick leave, no vacations. If there should be applicants coming forth in response to this ad, I will gladly change my position instantaneously. In the absence of such applicants, I will continue to insist that professionals must be ancillary to parents in this area.

There is also the question of children's needs. It was especially the psychologists (notably Dale Meers and Luitgard Wundheiler) who repeatedly brought up this point in the discussion. The data on this are consistent: children need structure and continuity. For this reason, more than any other, there are no professional substitutes for the family.

Thus I must argue with Sidney Callahan's understanding of the underlying disagreement at the conference. It is *not* an issue of individual rights versus family rights. Rather, the issue is what *social context* is most conducive to fostering the development of individuals. This is the hidden agenda of the current debate over children's rights. It is misleading to see this as an issue of the individual child versus the family. Young children are not able to take responsibility for their lives; there will always be adults who take responsibility on the children's behalf. But who are these adults to be? It is hard to see how the cause of individual rights is furthered by replacing parents with assorted professionals in this role. Of course there are cases in which parents must be replaced. Current laws provide for this. But it is a fundamental mistake to make these relatively rare cases normative for public policy.